HOW TO OBJECT TO A PLANNING APPLICATION OR PLANNING APPEAL

This book provides common sense and well-informed advice to anyone who needs to object to a planning application in England. It fills a gap in the market because it speaks to both lay and specialist audiences drawing on a lifetime of professional training, experience and teaching. The information and guidance is up-to-date, robust and effective, outlining an approach that can help the reader successfully object to poor quality planning proposals.

Joe Doak, Associate Professor of Urban Planning & Development (1992–2020), Henley Business School, University of Reading

Christian has been an invaluable Consultant over the years, with his in-depth knowledge of planning helping several of my clients to navigate their way through the planning system. It's great that he's been able to condense the salient points of that experience into these easy to understand guides, to enable people to engage with planning departments to good effect.

Tony Grover, BDS Surveyors

Christian is an intelligent and pragmatic town planning expert, and his many years of experience are evidence in this helpful and practical handbook. In my experience Christian's advice has been invaluable, if you cannot benefit from his service in person then you can benefit from this useful handbook.

Noël De Spéville L.L.B Solicitor

I have known Christian Leigh for the last 15 years during which time he has helped us on numerous occasions. Four times he has helped us shape arguments that have defeated inappropriate planning applications in our road and once he was able to help us acquire planning permission to build our own house on a challenging and narrow plot. His profound knowledge of planning statutes and the way the council process their decision making is invaluable when constructing irrefutable argument to make a point or challenge an assumption. Christian has succeeded in every situation we have used his services.

Mr S McNair, Berkshire

Christian's work for us in objecting to development near our home was invaluable, and this book is a great guide for how to be involved in the planning system

Mr & Mrs Baker, Berkshire

How to OBJECT to a planning application or planning appeal

A STEP BY STEP GUIDE

TO GETTING YOUR OPINIONS HEARD

2020 edition

Christian Leigh MPhil, MRTPI
Chartered Town Planner

ESSENTIAL tips to maximise your chance of **SUCCESS**

www.peculiaritypress.com

ISBN 978-1-912384-10-5

This work first published 2020
by Peculiarity Press, an imprint of Leigh & Glennie Ltd.
The Business Centre, Greys Green Farm, Henley-on-Thames
RG 9 4QG, UK.

Contents

Preface

Planning applications can affect everyone, wherever they live in the country. Planning permission is needed for development on land and at buildings, as well as the change of use of land and buildings. If a planning application is concerning you then this book sets out how to make an effective objection to the planning department and planning committee. A planning department will receive hundreds or thousands of planning applications a year. That leads to many objection letters coming to planning officers. You want to make sure your letter is clearly written, to the point, stands out and provides legitimate reasons to support your case. Similarly, planning committee members are likely to sit through many hours of meetings a year, listening to scores of people put their case. You need to ensure your case comes across well, with persuasive arguments.

You may also be faced with a planning appeal that affects you. Objecting at the planning appeal stage brings in different rules and procedures. There is also a different way to present your case to the independent Planning Inspector. As there are over 10,000 appeals a year, again you want to make sure your objection stands out and is persuasive.

This book covers the law and regulations for England, as there are differences in Wales and Scotland. It shows you how to make an effective objection to planning applications and appeals.

About the author

Christian Leigh is a chartered town and country planning consultant, with 25 years' experience working in private planning practice. His clients over the years include national housebuilders and development companies, many large and small businesses, as well as local and central Government.

He also works for numerous private clients and householders, as well as providing advice to architects, solicitors, surveyors and other professionals in the industry. This work has involved submitting many successful planning applications and appeals, as well as making representations on behalf of clients objecting to developments.

Christian is additionally a visiting lecturer in Planning Law and Practice at the Henley Business School, University of Reading, which is ranked No. 1 in the UK for Land and Property management.

1. Finding out about the planning application

In this section you will learn:

- The way in which the public are informed about planning applications.
- When you can write in to make your views heard about a planning application.
- What to do when you hear about an application.

Planning permission is required for development which, in brief, includes new buildings, extensions, works to buildings, and the change of use of land and buildings. In some instances, though, a specific grant of planning permission is not required from the Council (or local planning authority, LPA, as properly termed, and as used in this book). This is because the Government has decided that some forms of development is termed 'permitted development' and so does not need a specific planning application and grant of permission from the LPA. Most commonly this is for extensions to houses up to a certain size, small alterations to buildings and some changes of use. If work falls within permitted development then you are unlikely to be informed of those changes prior to work starting as no planning application is necessary.

However, if a development falls outside the definition of permitted development then a planning application to the LPA is needed. Once an LPA receives and validates a planning application they must publicise this. Surprisingly, this can be quite limited. The LPA is obliged to either write to neighbours most closely affected, or put up a site notice (a physical notice typically attached to a post or fence near the application site). They are not obliged to do both, though many LPAs do.

LPAs also vary widely in how many neighbours they directly write to. This may be a wide area, but sometimes it is only those directly adjoining.

This means that there is a chance you may not find out about a planning application. All planning applications are registered on your Council's website, and many now offer a service via their website to be kept informed about planning applications in your neighbourhood. It is worth signing up to that service if it is offered. Otherwise, you will have to trust to be notified, and to keep an eye out for site notices in your local area.

Anyone is entitled to write to an LPA setting out their views on a planning application, regardless of whether they were directly notified or not. This means that if you think other neighbours may be interested in a planning application and write in to object, then you can tell them yourself. There is more advice on how to do this later in this book.

TIME LIMITS

It is important to understand the timetable for planning applications.

The first point to be aware of is that once a planning application has been validated by an LPA they have a set period of time to determine it. This is usually within 8 weeks, but for major applications is 16 weeks. However, this does not mean that an application will definitely be decided at that 8 week (or 16 week) deadline: it may be after, or before.

The second point is that, once a planning application has been validated, the notifications sent out by letter/site notice allows for 21 days (3 weeks) to make representations. If you receive a letter from the LPA inviting you to write in then it will give a deadline for writing that refers to that 21 days. The LPA is not allowed to make a decision on the planning application within that 21 day period. This means that a decision on the planning application can be made anytime between 3 weeks and 8+ weeks.

In practice, most LPAs will not make a decision immediately after the 21 days (3 weeks) period of public consultation; a Planning Officer will obviously want some time to read everything that has been submitted during that 3 weeks before coming to a conclusion on the application. This means that you can write in with an objection after the 21 days deadline; the law requires an LPA to take into account any representations made before the formal date of decision.

This is a common misconception amongst objectors: that an objection can only be submitted within the 21 days, and anything later than that date will not be considered. However, there is a risk in submitting after that 21 days. Firstly, the Planning Officer may be quick in decision-making, and so after those 21 days have passed a decision could lawfully be made at any time. Secondly, you want to try to influence the Planning Officer, and so there is an advantage in getting your case in early. For example, if a Planning Officer has read everything to do with a case and come to a conclusion and then, a day before a formal decision is to be issued, your letter comes in, then unfortunately it is human nature that they may be less disposed to change their viewpoint at that very late time.

It is therefore advisable to make your objection within the 21 days in order to be certain your objection will be read, and to seek to influence the process at the outset. But if you have missed that deadline then you should still write.

REVIEWING THE PLANNING APPLICATION

This may seem an obvious point, but can be forgotten: make sure you fully understand the planning application. You do not want to write to object to an application and your objection be undermined as you have not properly understood the proposals, or made incorrect assumptions. The planning application will be available to view on the Council's website. It can be difficult to view everything online with pdf drawings and documents. Print out the drawings and key reports. Many LPAs will still enable you to view hard copies at the Council offices, so you can go in to view them there.

When you have understood the proposals, visit the application site, even if you think you know it. It is surprising the number of objectors who raise a concern with an application that is not actually there, eg that certain trees are to be removed when in fact the applicant has taken care to retain trees, or that an access to the road has poor visibility when there are clear views. The error comes because the objector's memory is not right, or they have not read the application drawings properly. If you make mistakes in your objection then your whole submission might appear incredulous, and your legitimate arguments might be undermined.

KEY POINTS

- The obligation for LPAs to notify neighbours directly about planning applications is quite limited. You may not be directly told, so keep a check on any public notices and on the LPA's website.
- Anyone can write in about a planning application, so if you have found out about an application that is of concern, you can tell your neighbours.
- The 21 day deadline for writing to the LPA is not an absolute deadline: you can write in after that.

2. Writing an objection letter

In this section you will learn:

- The importance of local and national planning policies when writing your letter.
- What to include in your letter, and what not to include.
- How to get support from others.
- What to do after submitting your letter to the LPA.

Having been informed of the planning application and thoroughly reviewed the submission, and all the supporting documents and drawings, now is the time to set out your objection.

Councils vary in how they want to receive objections. Some will request it be done online via a form, others emailing to a general email address, and some can still require the traditional letter in the post. Whatever method, ensure your representation includes the planning application reference number, the address of the application site and your own name and address. It is not unknown for a letter to go astray in the planning office and you do not want it ending up in the wrong file, or ignored.

FOCUS OF THE LETTER

Whilst there are no restrictions about what you can write in a letter, the LPA can only make a decision based on matters relevant to planning. You therefore want to avoid discussing irrelevances and concentrate on the key issues.

Before looking at the specific issues that might be addressed, it is important to think about the focus of the letter. That should be on planning policies, as it is against those that the planning application will be assessed.

The development plan

The law states that the decision on whether to grant planning permission must be made in accordance with the development plan, unless material considerations indicate otherwise.

This means that planning permission can only be granted by the LPA if they are satisfied that the proposed development accords with planning policies. If the LPA concludes the development does not accord with those policies, then permission must be refused, unless there are particular circumstances that allow for a departure from those policies.

Your objection letter must therefore seek to persuade the Planning Officer at the LPA that the planning application does not satisfy the policies relevant to the application. This is an element that can be overlooked by objectors. Simply saying why you do not want permission to be granted may be successful, but a good objection letter will tie that opinion to the development plan policies.

The development plan is the general term for what may be a whole host of differently named plans produced by the LPA, and also possibly by County Councils or regional authorities such as the Greater London Authority. The LPA, and all other authorities, review and update their plans over time. Once a plan has gone through all the procedures of consultation and review it becomes 'adopted'. As plans are reviewed at different times, there will be different dates for adoption to plans. These plans may also have varying titles, such as a Local Plan, or a Core Strategy, or a Development Management Plan, and may also include a Neighbourhood Plan.

You will be able to see the development plan policies on the Council's website. It is important to read these as they set out what will, and will not, be granted planning permission. Often the policies are worded rather generally. Policies concerning neighbouring amenity or design, for instance, often contain general aspirations to seek to ensure there is no loss of amenity for existing residents, and that new development is of a high standard of design. But many policies will have specific criteria against which development proposals will be tested. For instance:

- policies relating to extensions may set out numerical thresholds that the LPA do not wish to see breached: dimensions might be given relating to the maximum depth or height of an extension
- certain geographical areas may have policies that set criteria for development, eg the LPA may allow for a particular increase in the floorspace of houses in the Green Belt, or have a policy that sets out a particular density of development in residential areas designated for their spacious character.
- policies relating to the change of use of commercial premises may give thresholds for the number of a certain use, eg they might define a shopping centre and state how many shops they wish to see in that area
- policies may show areas within a town where a certain density of development is sought, or particular uses resisted

The list of potential policies is almost endless. Yet, if the policy is relevant to the planning application then the LPA must determine the application against that policy. You therefore need to be aware of it and, if you think the planning application conflicts with that policy, set out why you believe there is that conflict.

Supplementary Planning Documents

As well as the policies in the development plan an LPA may have produced supplementary planning documents. These may appear in a variety of formats and are produced to provide additional information on a wide range of topics. Typically they concern the design of buildings and extensions, highways and parking, and development in conservation areas. They can be very detailed in their content, setting out strict requirements that LPAs often want to see met in precise detail.

These documents will be available on the LPA website and you should see if there is any support in these to object to the planning application. There is no obligation, though, for LPAs to produce this sort of document, so there may not be any publications.

National planning policies

There are other planning policies that may be of relevance, in addition to those of the development plan that are set out by the LPA. A principal consideration may be those produced by the Government, set out in the National Planning Policy Framework (NPPF). This is accessible via the gov.uk website. The NPPF is the overall strategic policy framework for England and Wales, and so all planning applications must be determined in accordance with the NPPF.

The NPPF sets out broad principles for planning in the country. However, it has been revised over the years since it was first published in 2012 and increasingly covers more detailed matters that may be relevant to a planning application.

An LPA's development plan should be in conformity with the NPPF, but there remain some development plans that have not been updated since the NPPF was published. This means the NPPF might contain policies that help in your objection. If the planning application appears consistent with a development plan that pre-dates the NPPF but conflicts with the NPPF, then it can be argued that the NPPF should take priority. If you think that should be the case then make that point as it could be a strong point.

The Government has also published Planning Practice Guidance, which is also accessible via the gov.uk website. This supplements the NPPF and wider planning procedure. It covers an extensive range of topics, and often gives advice on the interpretation of policies and processes to be followed. As with the NPPF, this may be useful to your objection and can be cited.

WHAT TO INCLUDE

Whilst the potential list of topics for an objection letter is almost endless, there are common topics that arise in objection letters.

Visual impact and design

This is a common concern. It may be from a house extension, where you see it is poorly designed for the area or house itself. Or it may be from a larger development, say an estate of houses, where it would fill in an open space that is important to the character of a village, or intrude into the landscape character of the countryside.

It will be helpful to first explain what is the existing character of the area. Is it one with a consistent appearance of buildings in terms of architecture or the type of bricks? Are heights of buildings very similar, or the front building lines? Do open pockets of space make a spacious character to the area? Or are you concerned with a wider countryside area, where fields form part of an attractive landscape? Whatever it may be, you should set the scene first: it is trickier to make the case that there is harm to an area if you have not actually said what characterises that area. You might use photographs with your submission to help show this.

Having set the scene, then be specific in where you consider the harm arises. Is the row of three new houses too tall or positioned forward of the building-line in an area of homogeneity? Is there a flat roof to the side extension when everywhere else has pitched roofs? Would building four houses in the rear garden result in houses and gardens that are obviously much smaller than the spacious character of the wider area?

The key idea is to convey what you consider is important as the character of the area, and why. The Planning Officer may not know the area, nor local Councillors on the planning committee. Then tie your objection to that assessment.

Overlooking and loss of privacy

The usual test in considering a planning application is whether there would be an unreasonable loss of privacy. Some degree of overlooking can typically be expected, particularly in an urban environment. For instance, in a pair of semi-detached houses or a row of terraced houses the first floor bedroom windows will look down into next door's garden. Or views between the windows are possible in the houses facing each other across a road.

Therefore, if a planning application proposes to introduce a window where there is not one already then do not automatically assume it cannot be permitted. Be objective. Is that window going to lead to a clear degree of overlooking that is unreasonable? Or is it in fact distant enough, or at such an angle, that although you can see it your privacy is not really harmed? A bedroom window may also be seen as not causing so much overlooking as, say, a living room window as it will be used less.

If you think there will be unreasonable overlooking then your objection should be specific on the change to the amount of privacy you currently have. Is the area of your house or garden completely private at the moment? How do you use that area, eg is it a bedroom or living room, or perhaps the private patio area directly next to your house, rather than just the rarely-used end of a long garden? How far away is the new window and what is the room behind?

If loss of privacy is a particular concern then include a request in your letter for the Planning Officer to view from your home. However, planning officers are very busy and cannot always arrange specific site visit times to neighbours, or you may be out when they happen to visit the application site. For this reason photographs showing the existing private situation and where the new windows would be can be helpful in case the Planning Officer cannot visit your home. You might choose to prepare a mock-up on your photograph of where new windows would appear. Only do this if you are confident that it will be accurate and is a fair mock-up, as if you make an error it will greatly undermine your case.

Overbearing impact and loss of light

These two issues are similar as they both potentially occur when there is new built development close to your garden or house, but there are important differences.

Overbearing is whether a new building, such as an extension to your neighbour, is too dominant to the outlook from your house or garden, such that it feels oppressive, or outlook is harmed, or feels over-dominant just due to the sheer presence of that building.

Whether something is overbearing is a matter of judgement. But, like the effect on privacy, the test will be whether there is an unreasonably overbearing impact. Whilst you may see a new extension at your neighbour, that in itself is not necessarily the same as the extension being overbearing. You have no absolute right to a view. You should therefore again be objective before raising this as a concern as you will need to be demonstrating that, despite there being that no right to a view, the development is in fact so obtrusive as to be harmful.

It is therefore legitimate for you to set out your own opinion on whether a proposal would be unreasonable. As with an objection on privacy you need to explain the current situation and then be specific in how the proposed development would unreasonably impact on this. Is the development too close? Too high? Or both? Is your neighbour's proposed new garage next to your window or patio which you use regularly, rather than just behind shrubs in part of your garden you do not regularly use? Again, you can ask the

Planning Officer to view the site from your property, but consider submitting photographs as well.

Loss of light is a more technical matter. The LPA may have published guidance on this, most typically in a supplementary planning document. These may set out certain criteria to be satisfied for new development, such as angles of view taken from adjoining windows that must not be breached in order to ensure no loss of light. If the planning application breaches those guidelines then that may well indicate a loss of light occurs, and you should highlight that to the Planning Officer.

The criteria in LPA's documents, though, tend to be fairly generalised as they cannot deal with every circumstance. This means that even if, on the face of it, an application complies with the guidelines, if you think there is going to be harm then you can still make your objection. For instance, your neighbour's extension might have been drawn up to the absolute limits of the LPA's guidance. But if the rooms in your house are already quite dark then perhaps you will notice any reduction and it would be harmful? Or maybe there is a difference in ground levels or a high fence between your two properties that haven't been picked up in any assessment, which means the impact on light would actually be much greater than anticipated.

A full assessment of the impact on daylight and sunlight can only be undertaken with a full report undertaken by a specialist. The applicant may have done that, in which case it will be submitted with the application. You can appraise that yourself and, if you think there are errors or unreasonable assumptions, then point that out. You can of course also commission your own independent consultant to do that.

Noise, disturbance and smells

Many types of development lead to the potential for noise; a new use for a building, longer opening hours for an existing building, or new patterns of traffic or deliveries, for example. If these concern you then explain exactly what the harm is compared to the existing situation.

As with the points on other amenity issues, the test will be whether there is unreasonable disturbance; you cannot necessarily expect an absolute ban on noise. This means you should explain the existing situation, and then specifically set out why the change is unreasonable.

For instance, if there is new housing in the rear garden at your neighbour with an access road, then you might be concerned with the noise from that road and vehicles turning and parking. You will need to explain the existing situation, the particular position of that road, where vehicles turn, where they park, why you are concerned if there is inadequate screening, etc, and how that all relates to your own quiet garden area.

Or there may be a proposal to convert a building to a shop near your house. If you think there would be disturbance from this then be specific in that objection. How far away is the shop and where is the entrance door for customers who might cause noise when leaving? Where is the delivery area for vehicles, or where will the bin store be? How do these areas relate to the bedroom windows in your house, or your quiet garden? What are the proposed hours of opening for the shop and for any deliveries? Are those reasonable given the surrounding area, eg if it is predominately residential, or if it is actually already quite mixed?

Disturbance may also come from sources other than noise. Fumes from cooking are common complaints from restaurants and takeaways. Details of any extract flues should be submitted and you should check that these are properly prepared with full details to show how odours would be removed, and that extract fans do not cause vibration disturbance. Are all the details fully justified, or are there just vague intentions to resolve these points later?

Trees

Removing trees as part of a planning application, or damaging trees during construction, are common concerns for neighbours and for LPAs. Similarly, LPAs will be aware of the need that retained trees are protected in the long term after any development has been built. The risks to trees in the longer term can arise from buildings being too close to trees and so harming their roots or long-term growth, or because future residents want to cut down or heavily prune trees.

For these reasons, if there are trees on an application that might be affected by a development then the LPA usually requests the applicant to submit a tree report. However, this is not always the case, and on small-scale applications such as extensions to houses this information may be missing. If you are concerned with the direct impact on trees through being removed, or the impact in the longer term, you should raise it.

If the applicant has submitted a tree report then read it carefully. There may be mistakes or assumptions made, or you may disagree with the conclusions. Are the trees as described? Do the trees shown to be removed have visual amenity value to the area? Are too many being removed? Would the access road shown cross the root protection areas of trees, and are there adequate measures to protect those trees?

Also consider the long-term issues of the trees. Are you concerned that new houses or an extension would be so close to a retained tree that future residents would have a poor outlook, so want to remove that tree or heavily prune it? In which case you might be arguing the tree is as good as removed in the future.

The LPA will have their own tree officer to assess these matters. If this is a particular concern you can seek your own specialist advice from an arboriculturist who can prepare a detailed assessment of the case.

Ecology

Certain species have protected status. If the planning application is likely to have an effect on species then the LPA should have requested the applicant to provide detailed ecological information on this topic. If you dispute their technical evidence then it is likely you will have to provide some similarly technical evidence to prove that; it is unlikely to be sufficient just to say you disagree with an ecologist's report.

But the LPA and the applicant may be unaware of protected species or an important habitat. If you, as a near neighbour, have evidence of ecological interest on the application site then you should inform the LPA of this. However, again it is important to back up this with proper evidence. Merely saying that you are concerned with the effect on, say, birds and reptiles, is unlikely to be given much weight by the Planning Officer unless you can provide definite evidence to support that claim.

Flooding

If a site is liable to flooding then the LPA will usually have requested a flood risk assessment (FRA) from the applicant. These should be detailed studies which review technical data and relevant statements on flood risk in the area. But if the submitted FRA seems deficient then you can raise this in your letter. Local knowledge about past flooding events and the lie of the land is relevant to appraising the risk of future flooding, so if a claim in the FRA is questionable then it is legitimate to say so.

Parking and servicing

The LPA will have published car parking requirements for new developments. If the planning application meets these requirements it will be hard to argue against the scheme. Be aware that parking requirements can be low - for housing it is often one space per dwelling, or even no parking spaces - as many LPAs seek to deter excessive car ownership. Parking standards will be contained within the LPA's development plan or supplementary planning documents on their website.

But even with this low requirement, an application may still be seeking to provide fewer spaces, in which case the applicant should have argued why a lower provision is shown. If you think there should be a higher number of spaces then you need to explain why. Is there existing high pressure in the area for on-street parking? If future residents in a house have no parking is it really feasible that they can get around without a car, eg are there bus routes in the area and local shops?

The LPA will also have standards for servicing of new developments, such as access for lorries to serve shops or other commercial premises. But if your local knowledge means you are concerned with the arrangements then you can point out why, in this particular instance, the standards are not sufficient to ensure safe servicing. Or the applicant might be proposing unsocial hours for servicing into late night or at weekends. You can point out your objection to this.

Highway safety

The Highways Authority will be consulted on the planning application, which is the Council's technical body that reviews the details of the scheme with regards to whether access is safe, the roads in the wider area are safe and have capacity for the development, and whether the development would inconvenience other road users. If you have concerns on these matters it is likely they will need to be supported by firm evidence; generalised concerns about an increase in traffic, or that there is a new junction onto a road are unlikely to carry much weight.

There may be guidance on the Council's website that sets out the highways standards, such as the dimensions for junctions or new access points, or data on traffic levels in the area. However, this information can be patchy, and the technical appraisal can be complex. If highway safety is a particular concern then you may want to consider employing a highways consultant.

Effect on conservation area

If the application site is within a conservation area then the LPA has a particular duty to preserve or enhance the character and appearance of that area. If you are concerned that the planning application will be harmful then you should explain your objections in relation to that character and appearance of the area. The LPA may have published a study on the conservation area, which should be on their website. This will have appraised the conservation area to see what makes it important, and is quite likely to have then set out criteria to be satisfied by any planning application. For instance, how large extensions should be, what design features should be included (or avoided) in new buildings, sites or views within the conservation area where development should not occur.

Not all LPAs will have produced such detailed guidance, but if they have this is a very good ground for objection: if the application conflicts with the specific appraisal or guidance for the conservation area then you need to mention it.

Effect on listed buildings

If a development proposal involves a listed building then the LPA will have asked the applicant to also make an application for listed building consent. You may object to such an application in the same way as with planning applications, but clearly your objection will concentrate on how you consider the scheme would harm the architectural or historic interest of the property. This can be a specialist appraisal and you may want advice from an architect or historic buildings consultant.

However, even if a planning application does not directly concern a listed building, all planning applications must ensure there is no harm to the setting of a nearby listed building. This means that, for instance, a poorly designed or positioned new extension should not obscure views of a nearby important listed house. Or a proposed new access to serve a new house should avoid crossing over land that harms how an attractive listed house is seen in the wider street scene. It is therefore legitimate for you to raise concerns relating to the setting of a listed building if you feel the planning application would be harmful.

Existing experiences

If the applicant has caused you a nuisance in the past then in most instances this has little relevance. However, planning applications can be made to retain an existing development that is already occurring. If you have already experienced a development where permission is sought for its retention and it has been disruptive, noisy, unsightly, etc, then it is relevant to make that point: if the applicant is not proposing any substantive change on their property then why would there not continue to be harm?

Similarly if, say, a business wants to extend their premises or increase their working hours, then if they have been a poor neighbour in the past that may be relevant. Again, if they are not showing any firm controls on their activities then you may be concerned with disruption continuing even more in the future.

Precedent

If a similar development has occurred in the area that you think illustrates well the same harm you fear in the current planning application you are concerned with, then you might raise it in your letter. However, the danger of this is, of course, that it may demonstrate that the LPA have already granted permission for a similar scheme. For this reason you need to make sure you point out with evidence why another example is relevant, and harmful. For instance, if there is a proposal for a new house that is close to a tree you think might be harmed in the long term because it overhangs the house - even though the applicant says all will be fine - then if there was a very similar application for a house next to a tree that was later removed, then that may be relevant.

It is a principle in planning that every planning application is determined on its own merits. Therefore saying that granting a planning application will inevitably lead to more developments to which you are opposed may not be a strong objection. But this might be relevant in cases where, say, there is a very consistent character to the area. If a particular design of extension is permitted at a house within an estate of homogenous appearance, then if you are opposed to that design you may be concerned it would set a precedent for other houses to seek planning permission for the same design at a later date. Whilst the change to one house might be fairly minor, if many houses changed then perhaps the attractive character of that wider area would be harmed.

Material considerations

The general catch-all to many points in the planning system are material considerations. As mentioned earlier, planning applications must be determined in accordance with the development plan unless material considerations indicate otherwise. This broad term potentially means any topic might be weighed in the balance as to whether or not permission should be granted. But the requirement is that any other consideration must be material to planning, and relevant to the development proposed in the application.

The list of material considerations is potentially endless. They may include circumstances personal to the applicant - a person's need for a new development, or why a business needs to extend, for example - or there might be some particular fact in the case that just is not obviously covered by the normal policies in the development plan. The applicant may have raised a material consideration in their application in support of their proposal. If you disagree that this is relevant then you will need to clearly explain why. Similarly, if you think there are material considerations that indicate permission should be refused – in the face of what might otherwise appear to be an application consistent with the development plan – then you are entitled to raise those points, provided they are relevant.

WHAT NOT TO INCLUDE

There are certain matters that are not relevant to the decision-making process under the planning acts. Avoid putting these in your letter as they will divert the Planning Officer from reading what is really important in your objection.

The perceived loss of property value

The planning system is not concerned with the value of your house or land. Including an objection on this ground is a sure-fire way of coming across as objecting only for your own financial self-interests and should not be mentioned.

Private disputes between neighbours

Do not use a planning objection to air your grievances with your neighbour. The Planning Officer will not be interested in any dispute about fences or boundaries. The only exception to this is if the planning application proposes to build on land that you say you own. The applicant must serve formal notice on the owner of any land covered by the planning application, so if that has not been done – the application covers your land – then that can be drawn to the attention of the LPA.

The loss of a private view

The planning system does not seek to protect private views from, say, your bedroom window or garden across a field. This is different from protecting public views, for instance a view seen from the pavement along a street towards an attractive, rural churchyard; such a public view is a legitimate consideration.

The impact of construction work

Noise and disturbance during construction work is rarely a consideration, as control over any unreasonable impact is covered by other legislation. However, some LPAs do attach planning conditions to the grant of planning permission for certain types of development with particular likelihood for disturbance, such as subterranean development, or new-build development in locations close to existing properties due to the potential for disruption. But this is rarely a ground for refusing permission; the conditions are there to limit disturbance.

Issues covered by building regulations

Many detailed matters are controlled by other regulations, principally building regulations, such as fire safety, drainage, sewerage, structural stability. These matters are rarely relevant to the decision to grant planning permission, unless you can specifically demonstrate the design, layout, use etc of a proposed development is so deficient as to mean these matters could not be controlled through the normal building regulations.

Competition between firms and need

The need for a new use or type of development is usually not relevant in the decision about whether to grant permission. Nor can the LPA take into account whether a new development might have a harmful effect on other nearby businesses. Hence, even if you think there are too many coffee shops in an area, or that a new chain supermarket might affect a nearby small retailer (or your own shop) then that is not in itself a ground for refusing permission.

There can, though, sometimes be an exception to this rule. The development plan might set out limits for a particular type of use in a particular area. For instance, to ensure an existing town or village centre remains predominately a centre for shopping, then the LPA may have set out in their development plan that they will refuse permission for non-retail uses once a certain threshold is reached; say, to resist estate agents or betting shops above a certain level. If there are policies that set out such an approach then this line of objection might be relevant.

Land ownership, disputes over rights of way, restrictive covenants

In general, the LPA are not concerned with matters of land ownership, rights over land or any covenants that might exist on land. An applicant is in fact allowed to make a planning application on land they do not own, provided they follow the correct procedure in notifying the land owner that such an application has been made. The LPA will therefore generally take the view that, if there is some private agreement, restriction or covenant on the use or disposal of land, then that is a matter that the various landowners will resolve; it does not come under planning legislation. For instance, if an applicant wants to build a house on an area of land and you believe there is a private covenant from another landowner restricting that, then the LPA can still grant planning permission. It is between the applicant and the landowner to resolve this.

There can, though, be some circumstances where land ownership or restrictions on rights are relevant. This is particularly the case for access. If, for example, an applicant has shown that safe access for vehicles is over land that he does not own, or the visibility splays for a new junction would cross over land not under his control, then it might be relevant to point that out to the LPA. Without that land then it may be the case that the new development is not safe, and there could be harm to highway safety. The LPA might then seek further information from the applicant, or might consider planning permission can still be granted subject to a suitable planning condition or legal agreement. Permission may therefore not be stopped, but you will have made sure that an issue that was of concern has been properly considered.

Personal morals or views about the applicant

Do not enter into any discussions about your own views on the applicant's motives for making the planning application, or on their morals or beliefs. Nor should you object on the grounds that the applicant is making the application for profit; the planning system is just the process whereby a company, such as a developer or local company, has to achieve the necessary permission in order to carry out their business.

Example letter 1

A planning application for a two storey rear extension to the rear of your neighbour's house, where you are concerned with the impact on your own house and garden.

A Smith
12 Acacia Avenue
Anytown
A12 3BC

15 February

FAO B Jones, Case Officer
Anytown Borough Council
Civic Offices
Anytown
A45 6DE

Planning application ref: AA/1234. 10 Acacia Avenue, Anytown

I live next door to the above property and write to set out my objections on the grounds of harm to overbearing impact, privacy and effect on trees.

Overbearing impact

The planning application is for a two storey extension to provide a new living room and bedroom for 10 Acacia Avenue. The extension would be positioned very close to the boundary between our properties, extending 5m in depth and 6m to the eaves. This would be overbearing to the outlook from my patio and from the window to my living room.

[You could expand on this part, including photographs of the existing situation.]

Policy H4b of the Anytown Local Plan states that extensions to dwellings will only be permitted if they do not harm the outlook for neighbouring residents. The Anytown 'Householder Extensions' Supplementary Planning Document provides a guidance for two storey rear extensions to be no more than 3m deep. The planning application breaches that guidance, and has a harmful impact.

Privacy

The design incorporates a new bedroom window at first floor level that would introduce new overlooking to my garden area.

[Again, you can provide more information and photographs.]

Policy H4c of the Anytown Local Plan resists extensions that are harmful to the privacy of neighbours. The clear overlooking of my garden would be contrary to that policy.

Trees

I have a large beech tree in my rear garden, which can be seen from neighbouring houses and the street and contributes to the character of the area. The proposed extension comes within the canopy of that tree and close to the trunk. There is no detailed information on the effect that the proposed extension may have on the tree during construction, or in the longer term. The Anytown 'Guide to Trees in Development' Supplementary Planning Document requires applications that might affect trees to be accompanied by a tree survey, and sets out guidance for the proximity of trees and extensions. The application does not comply with this guidance, and so conflicts with Policy T4 of the Anytown Local Plan that requires all developments to not harm important trees in the Borough.

Summary

The application would be harmful to my amenity, and to trees, and so is contrary to the development plan and to Supplementary Planning Documents. I ask that it be refused permission. Should the application be reported to Planning Committee then please inform me of the date, as I would wish to attend and speak.

Yours sincerely

A Smith

Example letter 2

A planning application for 5 houses on a site within a village, where you are concerned with effect on character, highways, flooding.

A Smith
18 Beech Drive
Anytown
A12 3BC

15 February

FAO B Jones, Case Officer
Anytown Borough Council
Civic Offices
Anytown
A45 6DE

Planning application ref: AA/5678. Land to the rear of 35-39 Beech Drive, Anytown

I live close to the above site and write to set out my objections on the grounds of a harmful impact on the character of the area, the impact on highway safety and parking, and my concerns regarding flooding.

Effect on character of the area

The planning application is for the demolition of one house and erection of 5 houses on land to the rear of existing houses fronting Beech Drive, with a new access road provided to the road. Acacia Road has a consistent character of two-storey stone houses that front the road, with steeply pitched slate roofs. The land behind the houses is open and undeveloped.

[You could add more to explain the character of the road and wider area, including photographs.]

The demolition of one house and creation of a small cul-de-sac of new houses would not reflect this character. The location of the houses to the rear and their setting around an access drive would disrupt the strong frontage of housing in the street. The new houses would be brick, with shallow-pitched tile roofs

[Add more on what is specifically the harm to the area from the proposal, compared to the existing character.]

Policy H1 of the Anytown Local Plan requires all new housing proposals to have regard to the context in which they sit, and to be of a high quality of design. The Anytown 'Character Area Appraisal' Supplementary Planning Document has identified this part of Anytown as being characterised by detached houses fronting the road, and set in spacious plots. The proposal would conflict with this policy and guidance.

Planning permission was refused for the erection of 3 houses to the rear of 75-77 Beech Drive last year (ref. AA/3456), which was partly on the grounds of harm to the character of the area due to the layout of the new houses. This current planning application would lead to the same harm, and so should also be refused. If planning permission was allowed then it is likely to set a precedent for other similar housing schemes to come forward, which would erode the recognised character of the area.

Impact on highway safety and parking

The proposed new access road would lead to additional vehicles turning onto and off Beech Drive. This is the main 'A' road between Anytown town centre and the motorway.

[You can provide details of the road and an indication of traffic along the road.]

There is a bus stop only 5m to the south of the proposed access, and parked cars along the road that will prevent good visibility from the access road.

[Provide details of any physical characteristics of the road that might be relevant, eg parked vehicles, a curve in the road, buildings or trees that obscure visibility.]

The five new houses would be harmful to highway safety. There would not be clear visibility for turning vehicles and these dangerous manoeuvres would be onto a busy road. The proposal would therefore conflict with Policy M2 of the Anytown Local Plan that requires all development proposals to not be harmful to highway safety.

The proposed five houses are shown with one car parking space per house, and two visitor spaces. This is short of the parking standards set out in Policy M3 of the Anytown Local Plan. The likely result of this is that new residents will try to park on Acacia Road, which is already heavily parked. This will lead to traffic congestion in the area and is contrary to the planning policy.

Effect on flooding

The application site is partly liable to flood from the brook at the rear of the site. The applicant has provided a Flood Risk Assessment that says the new houses would not be at risk of flooding, or cause any off-site flooding risk. However, their Assessment assumes there has not been flooding on the land in recent years, and also does not take into account the proposed raising of land for the new access road. I enclose photographs of flooding across the area from last winter.

[The strength of an objection on a technical ground clearly depends on whether you have evidence to contradict the appellant's evidence, or if they have made an error in their submission. If so, you need to explain specifically why the applicant is wrong in any conclusion on a technical matter.]

Policy F2 of the Anytown Local Plan requires all development to not be at risk of flooding, or to increase the risk of flooding elsewhere. The evidence indicates that this policy would not be satisfied.

Summary

The application would harm the character of the area and to highway safety. There would also be harm to flooding in the area. The Council have recently refused permission for a similar development in the vicinity, and the current application is contrary to the development plan and to Supplementary Planning Documents. I ask that it be refused permission. Should the application be reported to Planning Committee then please inform me of the date, as I would wish to attend and speak.

Yours sincerely

A Smith

Example letter 3

A planning application to extend an existing takeaway and change the opening hours, where you are concerned regarding the potential noise and the visual impact of an extract flue.

A Smith
20 Chestnut Hill
Anytown
A12 3BC

15 February

FAO B Jones, Case Officer
Anytown Borough Council
Civic Offices
Anytown
A45 6DE

Planning application ref: AA/7890.
25 Chestnut Hill, Anytown

I live next to the above property and write to set out my objections on the grounds of the impact on my amenity and the visual impact of the proposed extract flue.

Noise and disturbance

The existing takeaway is open until 11pm on weekdays and to 11.30pm on Saturdays. The planning application seeks permission to build an extension to the rear of the property to enable a larger kitchen, and to increase the opening hours until midnight on weekdays and on Saturdays to be open until 1am the following morning. The existing takeaway use already causes noise and disturbance due to customers coming and going, customers hanging around outside, and vehicles arriving and waiting. This has been until midnight on some occasions, as the applicant has not been keeping to the permitted opening hours.

[If relevant, explain the details of why there is disturbance from an existing use of land or premises, to indicate why you are concerned with proposals to use that land more intensively.]

The proposal to further increase the opening hours of the takeaway would be harmful to my amenity. My bedroom windows face the street and the takeaway, as well as the delivery area at the rear.

[Explain exactly why there would be harm from the use, eg how your house is used, the proximity of buildings, the position of matters such as doors, windows or parking areas.]

There would be noise and disturbance later into the night when I should expect it to be quiet. The applicant's existing limited use of the premises until very late has been noisy, and so this should not become permanent. Policy D3 of the Anytown Local Plan requires commercial developments to not cause unreasonable disturbance to neighbouring residents. The extended hours would conflict with this policy.

Visual impact of the flue

The proposed extension to the building would be to the rear and, as this is a small extension and would not be visible from the street or my property, I have no objection to that.

[If there are elements of a planning application that do not concern you, then it is fine to point that out as it may indicate you are not objecting to everything for the sake of objecting.]

However, as part of the works there is a new metal extract flue from the side of the extension that would run up the side of the building, above ridge height. This is a large structure that would be unattractive when seen from the street due to its position, height and design.

[You can expand on exactly why a feature is at odds with the character of the area and the appearance of a building.]

The flue would also adjoin the listed building of 17 Chestnut Hill, which is an attractive Georgian house. The design and position of the flue would harm the setting of this listed building.

[You can explain further the impact on that building, with photographs if relevant.]

Policy D1 of the Anytown Local Plan requires all development proposals to be of a high quality of design. Policy L3 resists development that would harm the setting of listed buildings. The proposed development would be contrary to those policies.

Summary

The application proposes longer opening hours for the takeaway. The use already causes noise and disturbance, and the applicant has on occasions already been operating for these longer hours, which has caused even more disturbance to me. I therefore object to these longer opening hours. The proposed flue would be visually intrusive. The application is contrary to the development plan and should be refused permission. Should the application be reported to Planning Committee then please inform me of the date, as I would wish to attend and speak.

Yours sincerely

A Smith

GAINING SUPPORT

Objecting to planning applications is not entirely a numbers game. A single well-argued letter can always influence the outcome. But undoubtedly the more letters of objection there are the better, as it shows there is more public feeling against the development. Also, some LPAs have policies in place that once a certain number of objections are made to a planning application then it must be determined by the planning committee, rather than an individual Planning Officer. This can be to your advantage, as explained in the next section of this book.

You should therefore try to organise others to write in on similar grounds to you. They should write individual letters: a petition is not usually a good idea as it is too generalised, and people tend to sign these with limited real thought about the issues. Thus, they usually are given little weight by the planning officers and the planning committee, and have the extra disadvantage of putting off people from writing their own letters; they think they have done their part by signing a petition.

Individual letters should be written in own words, so avoid standardised letters where an objector just signs their name at the bottom. If your neighbours and others need help a good idea is to give pointers to what to include, rather than drafting the whole letter.

Example of an invitation to support

A developer has put in a planning application for 8 houses on rear gardens at two houses. Rather than having one petition signed by 8 residents, or eight identical letters signed by the residents, you could write to set out your objections and then send a note to neighbours as follows:

Planning application ref: AA/4567.
Land to the rear of 6-8 Oak Street, Anytown

Dear Neighbour.

You may be aware of the above planning application near your home, which is for the erection of 8 houses on the rear gardens. You can see the plans for the application at the Council's website

[You can provide details of a direct link to the relevant page of the website here.]

I am concerned with the impact of this development and am writing to the Council to set out my objection. If you wish to object to the above planning application then please write to the planning department explaining why you object.

[Provide details on how to make an objection, ie where it should be sent in writing, or email, and the deadline for submission.]

The main reasons for objection seem to be:

- Effect on the character and appearance of the area. The new houses would be built on land currently open and undeveloped.

- Effect on trees. Six trees are to be removed, which can be seen from the road.

- Highway safety. A new access road will be created, crossing the pavement near the school.

[The list of points is obviously dependent on the case, but by summarising what you think are the main issues – and the reasons why there could be an objection – then other residents are directed to think about those points and be able to write their own opinions in their own words.]

Yours sincerely

A Smith

SUBMITTING YOUR LETTER

Once you have submitted your letter to the LPA that is not necessarily the end of your involvement in the application. Procedures vary by LPA, but most will put your objection letter on the website for the planning application. This means that the applicant is able to read what you have said, and so potentially can respond with their own written submission to counter your points, provide new evidence or amend the proposed development. Again, each LPA will vary in whether they accept such additional information or amendments from the applicant; some do not and simply determine the planning application on the basis of what was first submitted, whereas others are happy to allow negotiations and changes through the course of the application.

LPAs also vary in how they respond to additional information or amendments from an applicant. If an application has been amended significantly then it is likely the LPA will contact those who have already objected to let them know of the change, and a formal re-consultation period will start. But if there are only small changes, or if the applicant has just written with additional information or to rebut your objection, the LPA may not contact you.

This means that it is sensible to keep a check on the progress of the application once you have submitted your representation. If the LPA publishes all documentation on the website then look at that regularly – it is likely the applicant is doing the same – to see if there is additional information. It is important to remember that you are allowed to write in again. So, if the applicant has provided additional information that you feel needs a response, then you can make a further representation.

Similarly, another individual or organisation may have written in to the consultation period. For instance, the Environment Agency may have provided comments regarding flooding matters, or the Highways Authority provided evidence on traffic or safety. If, having read that new information, you feel that you can beneficially add to what they have said, then you are allowed to write in.

Your involvement in the planning application can also continue into the formal determination period, which is discussed in the next chapter.

KEY POINTS

- Planning applications must be determined against the policies of the development plan. You should see what policies are relevant to the planning application and explain in your letter how the application conflicts with those specific policies.
- National planning policy and guidance may be relevant to an application, as it provides recent statements of Government policy.
- The LPA may have published Supplementary Planning Documents and other guidance for planning applications. These can set out detailed requirements that should be met – if the development does not satisfy that guidance, then point it out.
- Be focused in your objection letter, and stick to objecting on planning grounds. Be specific in what you object to: provide details of other examples, if relevant, rather than just general objections. Do not refer to anything on the list of non-planning issues!
- Once you have submitted your letter of objection keep a close check on the planning application. You may not be informed of any additional information as the application progresses. But if the applicant responds to your letter, or amends the application, then you can write in again.

3. How planning applications are decided

In this section you will learn:

- The ways in which an LPA will formally decide whether to grant or refuse planning permission.
- How to make further representations to the LPA, and when to do that.
- How to prepare for a Planning Committee.

An LPA will receive hundreds or thousands of planning applications every year. This is on top of other duties they must perform, such as enforcement investigations, conservation work, tree preservation orders, preparing their development plan etc. Most planning applications are therefore determined under Delegated Powers, with only a small number going to a Committee.

The method of determination can affect your involvement in the planning application. There may be the further opportunity to make your voice known, so you should try to find out how an application is to be determined. You can do this by including a direct request in your original objection letter: to ask that you are kept informed if the application is to be considered by a Committee, rather than under Delegated Powers. But it is also a sensible idea to keep track on the progress of an application via the LPA website, which should tell you how an application is to be determined.

DELEGATED POWERS

Most LPAs will typically determine around 95% of applications under Delegated Powers. This means it is the Planning Officer him or herself who decides whether permission is granted or refused. The process will involve an internal review of the intention to grant/refuse by a senior Planning Officer before the decision is officially 'signed off'. There is no external review of the decision or involvement by Councillors or a committee.

An application determined under Delegated Powers offers you little chance to further influence the decision after you have made your initial objection letter. As mentioned earlier, a planning application can be determined by the LPA any time after the 21 days' public consultation period has ended. If that application is to be determined under Delegated Powers after an internal meeting you may not know when that occurs. This shows how it is important to be comprehensive in your initial objection letter and to try to get it submitted within the 21 days, in order to best get your case across; you may not have another chance to put your view.

If you are concerned that a planning application to which you are objecting may be approved under Delegated Powers then you can write to your local Councillor to ask them to have the application referred to a Committee. There is no guarantee this will happen – Councillors will receive many such requests – so your letter or email must set out clearly why you think this particular application deserves attention. For instance, local Councillors, as politicians, are always going to be particularly interested where there are cases of wider interest.

LPAs are not obliged to inform objectors about the outcome of a planning application, even if you have requested to be informed in your original objection letter. This is another reason to keep a check on the progress of the planning application since, as shall be explained later, if you consider there to have been an error in the decision-making process there are strict time limits to do anything about that.

COMMITTEE

The minority of planning applications therefore go to a Committee. The exact arrangement of how applications make their way to a Committee depends on the workings of the individual LPAs. They may have different terms: the Planning Committee, or the Development Control Committee, or the Neighbourhood Committee, or any number of names. Whatever Committee it is, it is made up from a selection of locally-elected Councillors (or 'Members') from across the full Council. They meet to discuss and vote on the application and their vote is the formal decision on whether to grant or refuse planning permission.

The LPA will have different criteria that determine whether an application will be reported to a Committee. Typically this occurs in the following circumstances:

- If there is sufficient public interest in the application. The LPA may have specified a threshold for this to occur. For instance, if there are over 5 objection letters then an application is reported to Committee. But other times it may be a matter of judgement by the individual Planning Officer.
- If a Councillor has requested the application go to Committee. Local Councillors are informed of planning applications and they can request any application go to Committee, even if that application would usually be determined under Delegated Powers.
- If the application is of a particular size or type. Planning applications that fall within the 'major' category usually go to a Committee. Some LPAs may have other types of application that they always take to a Committee, for instance telecommunication masts, power-generating schemes, applications relating to schools. Other applications may just be considered to be too finely balanced for planning officers to determine themselves, and so the Committee is asked to make that judgement.
- If an application involves Council interests. To avoid any accusations of bias, most LPAs will take applications concerning their own land

or development to a Committee, or any applications concerning a Councillor's own land or interests.

One slight anomaly is that even if a planning application falls within one of these categories – most notably the first two – then it may still not go to Committee. The application will usually only go to Committee if the Planning Officer considers it should be approved in the face of, say, objection from the public or the local Councillor seeking refusal. If the Planning Officer agrees with the objectors, ie that the application should be refused, then the typical procedure is to then refuse it under Delegated Powers. The thinking on this procedure is that there is nothing controversial to decide, so it can just be refused.

If you have written in to object to a planning application and it is going to a Committee with a recommendation from the Planning Officer that it should be approved then you should be informed by the LPA. However, as mentioned earlier, it is sensible to keep a check on the progress of the application via the LPA's website or by direct contact with the Planning Officer on this matter. The LPA will inform you of the time and venue of the Committee and the arrangements for any public speaking, and this letter will usually come from the Committee Clerk or the Council's Democratic Services department. You will also be told when the agenda for the Committee is made available on the website.

The Committee stage of a planning application is an important event, and it gives you a chance to affect the outcome. The planning application is being reported to the Committee with a recommendation to grant permission. But Councillors are not obliged to follow that recommendation. Councillors are elected to make decisions, not just to rubber-stamp reports, and they may be quite happy to come to a different conclusion. How to affect their decision is discussed next.

Review the Committee Report

Before anything else, you should read the agenda for the Committee meeting. The Planning Officer will have prepared a detailed report that sets out why the application is being recommended for approval. You need to know why the Officer has not agreed with your objections in order to target your further work in seeking to get permission refused.

Further representations to the Planning Officer

If you have any concerns with the Planning Officer's assessment, or new evidence to help your case or contradict the Officer's conclusions, then you can write again at this stage. As mentioned earlier, the LPA must consider any submissions up to the date of determining the planning application, and that date is the Committee. But do not use this stage in the proceedings to repeat absolutely everything you wrote before for the sake of it; you made the case, and the Officer has not agreed, so just reiterating the same points is unlikely to be any help. You need to focus on, for instance, any particular errors in the Officer's conclusions, where they may have misunderstood your views, or if you have additional information or evidence that might genuinely lead to a different conclusion.

For this reason, do not feel obliged to write. If you have nothing extra to add to the Planning Officer's reasoning then your time is better spent preparing to influence the Councillors (see below). However, if you do write to the Planning Officer then keep it fairly short – no more than two or three pages – and to the point. Do not question the Officer's competence or integrity, even if you are angry with the recommendation to approve. The planning system is often a matter of judgement and balance, so the Officer is likely to have just had a different judgement to you. Also consider very carefully before threatening any legal action or other procedural action (this matter is discussed later).

Contacting Councillors on the Committee

There have been differing views over the years about directly contacting Councillors serving on a Planning Committee about planning applications before an application is formally determined. You may find that your LPA has specific guidance on this, and you should check on their website or direct with the Committee Clerk to see if they have particular protocol. However, in general, most LPAs take the view that members of the public may wish to contact Councillors direct to set out their views on a planning application.

If you intend to do this then only write after the publication of the agenda for the Committee. As mentioned earlier, the Councillors on a Committee will come from across the Council area and so may not be aware of a planning application affecting your area until the agenda is published. They are busy people, so there is little point in telling them about the application until it is close to the meeting where they have to think about whether to grant permission.

Contact details for Councillors will be on your Council website. They usually have both an email and a postal address. Email is obviously quicker, convenient and cheaper. However, everyone has so many emails now that there is a risk that it is not seen. You may therefore want to revert back to the traditional way of sending a letter in the post as that can stand out more in this day and age. If you do that, though, of course ensure you leave sufficient time for it to be received and read before the Committee meeting.

As Councillors are busy, and will be considering a number of other planning applications at the same Committee, you need to make sure your email or letter is focused and short: with a letter try to get it down to a single page, or at most two. As with writing to the Planning Officer, do not question the competence or integrity of the planning department. Just concentrate on the main points why you think permission should be refused, contrary to what the Officer recommends. The points need to be related to planning, but think about what matters to the Councillors, who are the local politicians representing their individual Wards and the Council area. Avoid detailed technical appraisal which misses the most important issues you want to convey. Your full letter of objection that you previously submitted will be on the public file, so you should refer the Councillor to that so they can read more if they wish.

You should write the same letter to each Councillor and then send a copy of that letter to the Planning Officer. Make it clear to the Councillors that you are writing the same letter to all of them and also that you are sending it to the Officer. This is to avoid any possible perception that you are unduly trying to influence matters, and so both the planners and the Councillors know exactly what information has been seen by everyone. Do not expect any response from the Councillor, and certainly no indication as to whether they are minded to approve or refuse the application. That would lead the Councillor open to an accusation of pre-judging the application, and so they will usually avoid responding.

Attending and speaking at the Committee

Not all LPAs allow speaking at the Committee, but if they do then the letter informing you of the meeting will have told you this. The letter will set out the process to register for speaking, which usually involves phoning or emailing a particular person at the Council offices by a deadline. Ensure you do this correctly as any deadlines are rigorously enforced. You can register to speak yourself or it is acceptable to employ an advisor to speak, such as a planning consultant, a solicitor or other specialist as might be needed.

You should also find out what the process is if there is more than one objector who wants to attend and speak. Again, different procedures apply in different Councils. Some allow multiple speakers to speak in objection, others only allow one. If it is the latter then some Councils will just allow whoever registered first, whereas others provide objectors with others' contact details so they can liaise with speaking. If you know there may be more than one person speaking – and you want to be one of those – then it is sensible to discuss with other objectors before registration so you are properly coordinated.

You may also want to coordinate who is best to present the message you want to convey. There may be quite detailed planning policy or technical issues that need a firm and succinct response, in which case an objector (or a representative) could be best. Or the issues may be more local and heart-felt, where the passion of a local resident may better sway the local politicians.

Also find out what the process is for the presentation of additional information at Committee. Some LPAs will allow objectors to speak with reference to information such as drawings or photographs, but it is usual that these are submitted prior to the Committee to allow the Planning Officer or Chairman of the Committee to check suitability. However, some LPAs do not allow any further information to be presented, so do not necessarily expect this.

Once you are registered to speak at the Committee then you need to prepare in advance, and be ready for the evening itself. There are key dos and don'ts.

Dos

- **Be aware of time limits.** Different LPAs have different time limits for speakers. Typically it is three minutes, but some allow up to five minutes. If there is more than one speaker then check if the time limit is per speaker or to share; some LPAs allow, say, five minutes to be shared between a number of speakers.
- **Prepare and practise, and practise again.** Whatever the time limit is, practise beforehand that you will get your points across in that time. Time limits are strictly enforced and you will be stopped if you run over. Write down what you want to say and practise speaking. That may be the full speech or just notes, but whatever method you choose you must practise, and practise again. Overrunning speeches and garbled attempts to fit in the last 10 points or 2 pages of notes in the dying seconds are the most common reasons why objectors' speeches fall flat.
- **Be concise.** You may have many reasons why you object to the application, but you are unlikely to convey everything in just a few minutes. Concentrate on the main points, and those where Councillors

can legitimately take a different decision to the Planning Officer. And remember that you do not have to use every second of your time limit.

- **Be prepared to be flexible in what you say.** The usual order of speaking at a Planning Committee is that the application is introduced first by the Planning Officer, who summarises the proposal, usually with reference to the plans and photographs. Objectors usually then speak. Pay attention to what the Planning Officer has said and if you think that there are particular facts that need clarification or correction then mention it in your speech. A supplementary agenda may also have been produced at the Meeting (see below) which might raise a point that needs a response. This is another reason to make sure your speech is concise, and perhaps below the time limit, so you have some slack if you need to add a sentence or two.

- **Be prepared for questions.** Some LPAs simply allow you to speak and that is the end of your time. Others specifically allow for a time to be questioned by Councillors about your views, but in all events there is the possibility you may be asked for a factual clarification. Councillors may want to know more details about what you have said, or ask for you to explain more about your views. This can be probing, and so potentially unnerving. The best way to get through this is to prepare thoroughly. Re-read everything you have written before, and be very familiar with the planning application itself and the Planning Officer's report.

- **Arrive on time.** A simple point, but important. If you have registered to speak then you will have been told when to arrive, and if you need to report to anyone on the night. If you do not report at the right time you may not be able to speak. It is common for the agenda to be run in a different order to that published. Therefore, even if the application you are interested in is listed far down the agenda you should still report when asked as the item may have been moved to an earlier slot on the night.

- **Pick up a copy of the agenda and any supplementary papers at the Committee.** You will have seen the Agenda already from the Council's website, but there will also be printed copies at the meeting. There may well be printed copies of supplementary papers: a report on any relevant additional information that has been received by the Planning Officer since the date the original Agenda was published. This is very important to read as it may contain information or evidence that is relevant to your case, for instance new information about a proposed pattern of use, or the treatment of windows in an extension, or proposed planning conditions; the list of potential points is endless, but they may be significant to you. If you think this new material merits a response because, say, it is being presented by the applicant in an attempt to overcome your objection but you are still concerned then you should refer to it. Or the new information may have addressed one concern and so it may be sensible not to waste your time objecting on that point, eg if you were objecting to an extension on the grounds of loss of privacy from a side window, overbearing, light and design, and the supplementary papers reports an offer to have obscured glazing to that window then you would probably be best spending your time speaking about the other matters.

Don'ts

- **Avoid long-winded introductions.** Your time is limited, and there is no need to thank people or introduce yourself or others in detail, or describe the application, unless any of that is absolutely necessary.
- **Do not criticise process or the Council.** Objectors can feel angry about applications for many reasons that might not be related to the planning issues, for instance about multiple planning applications being made over time, or the lack of notification of a planning application, or that a developer seems to be ignoring local opinion. But the Councillors are there to consider the planning application and, whatever may be your concerns in the past, that is the simple fact for the Committee meeting. Venting your frustrations will use up time and is likely to make you appear as a general complainer, rather than putting a dispassionate case.

- **Avoid references to non-planning matters.** These were discussed earlier, but objectors frequently refer to building regulation and construction issues in their speeches, which are covered by other legislation. And particularly avoid talking about the effect on property values, as that can instantly make you appear motivated to object only for your own interest.
- **Do not try to hand out unexpected information.** You should have already asked well before the Committee date if any additional information such as photos or drawings could be submitted. You will not be allowed to suddenly produce extra information on the night to hand out if that has not been agreed beforehand, as that could be seen as being unfair to others as they will not have seen it in advance or been able to check accuracy.
- **Do not try to speak again.** The usual process in a Committee meeting is that, after objectors have spoken, the applicant has the right of reply and can speak to the Committee. The Planning Officer then may speak to clarify any matters - possibly in response to specific questions from the Councillors - and the meeting then moves to Councillors discussing the application before a formal vote. You do not have any further right to speak, and any attempts to interrupt or shout out will be frowned upon and put you in a bad light. You can only watch and trust that the decision you want is made by the Councillors, even if you think there are mistakes being said. However, it is sensible to keep notes on any speeches, questions or the debate after you have finished your speech in case there is a need to take things further in the future (as will be discussed later in this book).

After the speeches are made to the Committee and a discussion undertaken by Councillors then a formal vote is held. This will either be to follow the Planning Officer's recommendation to approve or to refuse permission.

If the Councillors vote to refuse then they will need reasons for that refusal, and the Planning Officer present at the meeting will usually advise on the wording for that. If the application is approved or refused by the Committee then that is formal decision by the LPA.

Councillors may follow an Officer's recommendation to approve, but in a different manner. For instance, they may attach additional planning conditions to the grant of permission, or seek some other additional controls to the permission.

A Committee may also occasionally vote to defer a decision. This may be for a variety of reasons but is typically when Councillors feel more information is needed for them to make a decision, or they may wish to visit the site. In this instance the application will be reported back to a later Committee as the formal decision as to whether to grant permission has not been given. You should be informed of this Committee again. Procedures then vary between LPAs as to whether you will be able to speak to the new Committee; some LPAs allow a further speech, others do not.

A Committee might vote to 'defer and delegate' a decision. This is a resolution to approve planning permission but that the formal sign-off for the approval is to be made by the Planning Officer. This usually occurs where the Councillors are content with the principle of granting permission but there is some technical matter that has not been resolved, most typically the signing of a legal agreement. The Planning Officers are therefore given authority to resolve that last procedural hurdle and undertake the formal grant of permission.

THE FORMAL DECISION NOTICE

Regardless of whether a planning application is determined under Delegated Powers or by a Committee, and whether it is refused or granted, it is not until a formal Decision Notice has been issued that the LPA has actually made its formal decision. LPAs vary in telling objectors what was the outcome of a planning application and when the decision was made, since there is no obligation for them to do so. The Decision Notice will be published on the Council's website and you should seek it out.

You should read the Decision Notice to ensure that, if you attended the Committee meeting, it contains what you expected. If it was refused do the reasons accurately reflect what the Councillors voted on at the meeting? If it was approved are the planning conditions correct? Were any extra planning conditions requested by Councillors added? If you believe there are errors or omissions then you will need to contact the LPA promptly.

If you have serious concerns regarding the way in which the LPA made the decision then the date of the Decision Notice is very important if you intend to lodge any formal challenge (discussed next).

KEY POINTS

- Most planning applications are determined under Delegated Powers. If this is likely to be the case then you will need to keep a close check on the progress of the application to ensure you make all your objections known before it is determined, or to ask a local Councillor to call the application to a Committee.
- If the application is to be determined at a Committee then this gives you a further opportunity to make representations. This can be direct to Councillors, provided you follow the correct procedure and are clear to all Councillors and the Planning Officer you are writing to them. Most LPAs also allow objectors to speak at a Planning Committee.
- If you are speaking at a Committee then prepare well. Practise your speech to make sure it is under the time limit: allow yourself some slack in case there are other issues that arise on the night of the speech, such as what the Planning Officer may say, or what is produced on a supplementary agenda.
- Focus on just a few main points in any speech at Committee. If the recommendation from the Planning Officer is to approve, think carefully about the areas where Councillors might realistically come to a different judgement and refuse the application. You cannot cover everything in the few minutes you have.
- Pay attention to what not to say in a speech, and do not try to hand out any extra information unless that has been agreed beforehand.

4. After the formal Decision Notice for a planning application

In this section you will learn:

- The possible outcomes of a planning application.
- What you can do, depending on those outcomes.

If planning permission is refused then the appellant has a statutory right of appeal. You may have the right to be involved in the appeal and that process is discussed in the next section of this book.

If planning permission is approved then, despite your objections, there is no right of appeal against the approval. The only exception to this is if there has been a serious error in law in the LPA's decision itself, or in the decision-making process. If that is the case then a legal challenge can be made to the High Court by making an application for a judicial review that seeks to quash the LPA's decision.

There are strict limits on the grounds for challenging an LPA's decision and the Court will only be concerned with legal matters. These are typically confined to matters such as whether there has been the proper legal interpretation of planning policies and case law, or whether there have been any serious omissions or oversights in the LPA's appraisal of the application. The Court may also be concerned with any failing in the LPA's processing of the application, such as proper consultation on the application or how the application was considered by Planning Officers or the Committee; as noted in the previous section of this book, your notes of a Committee or observations on the formal

Decision Notice may help to demonstrate if there was any error by the LPA in what the decision should have been and what was produced in a formal Decision Notice.

The important matter to remember is that the Court will not exercise its own judgement on the merits of a planning application. Even if you strongly disagree with the LPA's decision to approve permission, provided that decision was made without any legal error then the Court will not intervene and overturn that approval.

If you consider there has been a legal error then you should seek advice from a solicitor. It will be a costly process and you want to be properly advised of the chances of success. There are also strict deadlines for making the application to the High Court, which start from the date of the Decision Notice, and which must be met.

It should also be noted that if the decision to grant permission is quashed then it does not necessarily mean permission is refused; the Court will require the LPA to reconsider the planning application again. The LPA may then determine the application correctly – without any legal flaws – and reach the same decision to grant permission.

KEY POINTS

- **A refusal of planning permission gives a right of appeal to the applicant if they disagree with the LPA's decision. You may have the opportunity to be involved in that appeal process.**
- **There is no similar statutory right of appeal against the grant of planning permission for third parties on the grounds that you disagree with the LPA's decision. The grant of permission can only be challenged in the High Court on strict legal grounds and within a certain timeframe. You should seek legal advice if you wish to follow that route.**

5. How to object to a planning appeal

In this section you will learn:

- How the planning appeal system works, as it is different to how planning applications are determined by an LPA.
- How to make representations during the appeal process and what to include in those representations.

If planning permission is refused by the LPA, and the applicant does not agree with that decision, then the applicant has the right of appeal to the Government. The LPA's decision can be overturned and planning permission granted. An applicant can also appeal against planning conditions attached to a grant of planning permission, or if the LPA fails to make a decision within the required time period (usually 8 weeks).

Residents and other third parties can be involved in most appeals. However, there are strict procedures to be followed: timetables to be followed, documents that can (and cannot) be submitted, and the possibility of costs being awarded if procedure is not followed properly. This section of the book explains how to participate in the appeal process.

WHO DETERMINES A PLANNING APPEAL?

The appeal is a formal process, made under s78 of the Town and Country Planning Act 1990, and is to the Secretary of State for Housing, Communities and Local Government. It is therefore, in strict legal terms, the Secretary of State who is determining the planning appeal and has the power to overturn the LPA decision. However, in practice, most appeals are determined by an individual Planning Inspector appointed by the Secretary of State.

The appeals system, and the management of the Planning Inspectors, is operated through the Planning Inspectorate. This is an Executive Agency of the Government and they are based in Bristol. Once an appeal is lodged, a Case Officer will be allocated who will be the contact throughout the appeal process for all parties involved in a particular appeal: the appellant, the LPA and you.

The actual appeal, though, is determined by the appointed Planning Inspector. It is that one person who makes the new decision. Unlike the LPA, there is no committee or panel that sits to determine the case on a majority basis, or any 'signing off' of a decision by a senior manager. The process is technically a tribunal, and the Inspector's decision-making process is quasi-judicial in character. Therefore, at appeal you are looking to make your case to, and persuade, just one person.

There are some procedural differences in appeals, depending on the type of case. But essentially they are all determined in the same way. The appointed Inspector looks at the case afresh. They consider all the evidence presented at the time of the planning application, and the evidence presented with the appeal itself. The process is truly independent and impartial. The Inspector will have no ties to the LPA (they do not work for the LPA, nor even live in the area). Inspectors are very experienced, and may come from a range of backgrounds, such as town planners, architects, ecologists, surveyors, solicitors. The appeals system is highly regarded amongst professionals for its independence.

The Inspector, having reviewed the case, will make the new decision on the refused application (or conditions attached to a planning permission, or a non-determined application, if that is the case). They may agree with the case put by any party in the appeal, ie the LPA, the appellant, or any third party who has made submissions, and so may grant planning permission or refuse planning permission. They can refuse permission on different grounds to those put forward by the LPA. Each Inspector exercises their impartial judgement in coming to their decision. Their actions and decisions are, though, governed by the relevant acts of parliament, statutory instruments and case law.

The new decision is binding on all parties. If the Inspector grants permission for the proposed development, the appeal is allowed; if the Inspector decides permission should not be granted then the appeal is dismissed. Whatever the decision is, it can only be challenged through the courts on points of law, not just because one party disagrees with the Inspector's judgement.

FINDING OUT ABOUT THE APPEAL

If you wrote in to the LPA at the planning application stage then, if an appeal is lodged, the LPA will inform you. The notification from the LPA will tell you the date the appeal was made valid, the contact details at the Planning Inspectorate for making any submissions, the Planning Inspectorate's reference number (it will be different from the LPA's reference number), the procedure by which the appeal is to be heard and, crucially, the date by which any representations to the Inspectorate must be made.

You are allowed to make submissions at the appeal stage even if you did not write at the planning application stage (with the exception of Householder Appeals, as explained later). The details for where, when and how to make any submissions are the same as for those informed directly.

Once you are informed of the reference number for the appeal you can also keep track of progress on the Planning Inspectorate's Appeal Casework Portal: **https://acp.planninginspectorate.gov.uk** This provides a reminder of dates for the submission of documents, allows online submissions, and is where the eventual Inspector's decision is first published. You can also register on the site which enables you to watch a case.

PROCEDURES

Planning appeals will run through one of the following procedures. These depend on the type of application made to the LPA, the compexity of the case, and the choice of procedure by the LPA, the appellant and the Inspectorate.

Householder Appeals Service (HAS)

If the appellant's planning application to the LPA was for an extension or works to a single family dwellinghouse, or development within the curtilage of a dwellinghouse, then it will have been termed a Householder Application. Any appeal will then fall within the Inspectorate's HAS procedure. A 'prior approval' application for a single storey rear extension also falls within this category. The HAS procedure is a fast-track system and has limited involvement at the appeal stage, as will be explained later.

Commercial Appeals Service (CAS)

Certain small-scale applications for works to commercial premises, such as new shopfronts, also run through a fast-track system. There is limited involvement with the CAS procedure.

Written Representations

Any planning application that did not fall within the Householder Application category, or within the small-scale commercial application, can potentially be determined by the Written Representations procedure. This involves the exchange of written statements by the appellant and the LPA, and the opportunity for you as a third party to write in. There is also the right of reply to these statements for the appellant and LPA. The Inspector visits the appeal site, but determines the appeal solely on the basis of these written documents.

Informal Hearings

The Hearing procedure is similar to Written Representations at the outset, as it involves the exchange of written statements and the opportunity for you as a third party to comment. However, the appeal will see a Hearing which is an informal forum for discussion led by the Inspector, attended by the appellant, the LPA and any other interested parties. This gives a far greater scope for exploring the issues in the case. The Inspector will visit the site, and makes the decision based on everything in the written documentation and said at the Hearing and the site visit.

Public Inquiry

The Inquiry procedure is a highly formalised process. The appellant will have submitted an appeal statement with the lodging of the appeal, but during the course of the appeal they will be submitting further evidence to provide a more detailed case. The Public Inquiry itself is a formal event, similar to a court of law in some respects, where the appellant and the LPA usually have legal representation. You and other third parties can be involved in this process. The Inspector will again visit the site, and make the decision based on all the evidence from the Inquiry and written evidence.

WHEN AND HOW TO MAKE AN OBJECTION

The type of appeal procedure will determine how you can be involved at the appeal stage: when you can make any written submissions, whether you can appear in person, and the deadlines you have to keep to.

Householder Appeals Service/Commercial Appeals Service

Your involvement with an HAS or CAS appeal is very limited. Once an HAS/CAS is lodged by the appellant the process essentially involves the LPA's case file being passed over to the Planning Inspectorate. This is the application form and supporting documents, any representations made during the course of the planning application – including any letters that you will have submitted to the LPA – the Planning Officer's Delegated Report or the Planning Committee Report, and the formal Decision Notice refusing planning permission. No one has the opportunity to make any further submissions: not the appellant, the LPA or yourself.

Once the appeal is lodged the LPA has the responsibility to provide all the background documentation to the Inspectorate. They do this by submitting what is termed the 'Appeal Questionnaire'. This is literally a document setting out questions and a checklist to be completed by the LPA, which shows that all the required information has been forwarded. The LPA will inform you that an HAS/CAS appeal has been lodged at the same time as sending their Appeal Questionnaire to the Inspectorate.

One important question that can be of particular relevance to third parties is the LPA's response to a question regarding the Inspector's site visit. As mentioned earlier, the Inspector will always visit the appeal site itself. However, they are not obliged to visit any nearby land unless specifically asked to. If the planning application was refused permission on the grounds of harm to a neighbour's amenity then it may be helpful for the Inspector to view from that neighbour's property. The LPA can request this on their Questionnaire. However, they do not always do this.

If you think there is a particular need for the Inspector to view the appeal site from your property at the site visit then, once you have been notified of the appeal by the LPA, you could contact them to ensure they make this request to the Inspectorate on their Questionnaire. You will have to be quick, though, as the LPA must provide that Questionnaire within five days of the appeal's official start date. However, it will be up to the LPA to decide whether they want to request a view from your property; clearly, if they did not refuse permission on the grounds of harm to your amenity then they are unlikely to request the viewing from your land. You might also try to contact the Inspectorate direct, but it is up to the Inspectorate – and the individual Inspector – to agree to this.

Written Representations

The Written Representations procedure gives you better scope for involvement. As with the HAS, the case file at the application stage is sent to the Inspectorate, which will include any letters that you submitted to the LPA during the course of the application. But you are entitled to write to the Inspectorate with a new letter that sets out your views on the appeal. The notification of the appeal from the LPA will tell you by when such a letter must be submitted. You can also ask the Inspectorate directly to make arrangements to view from your property, if you think that is relevant.

The appellant has the opportunity to make a written reply to any representation you have made. You do not have any further right of reply after your own letter.

Informal Hearing

A Hearing also involves the case file being sent to the Inspectorate, and any letters you previously submitted to the LPA will be seen by the Inspector. The Hearing process then similarly allows you to write to the Inspectorate at the outset of the appeal, setting out your views on the appeal. The LPA will inform you of an appeal proceeding by way of a Hearing and how to make any submissions, including the deadline by when any submissions must be made. You can also be involved in the Hearing itself to expand upon your views, and to respond to the appellant's case verbally.

Public Inquiry

This process provides similar involvement to a Hearing, with the ability to provide both written submissions and verbal evidence at the formal Inquiry itself. Again, the letter of notification from the LPA will tell you how to make any submissions, and by when that must be done.

WRITING AN APPEAL OBJECTION LETTER

If the appeal is proceeding other than through the HAS/CAS routes, then you can write to the Inspectorate. Writing at the appeal stage is different to when you wrote to the LPA at the application stage. The Inspector will have received a copy of what you wrote to the LPA, so there is little point in just repeating everything you have already said.

The LPA will have set out what they consider to be the objections to the case on their formal Decision Notice and in their Delegated Report or Committee Report. The appellant will also have submitted their grounds of appeal with the lodging of the appeal. This means there is a lot of new information since you made your original objection to the LPA. The previous advice in Chapter 2 still applies about what to include, and not include, in your new letter. However, you also need to think about the following to inform what you include in your new submission to the Inspectorate.

Read the reasons for refusal

The Decision Notice from the LPA will have set out the reasons why planning permission has been refused. The detailed Delegated or Committee Reports (and minutes from any Committee Meeting) will provide more information. You should read these documents. You are likely to agree with the reasons and, as it was the LPA's judgement that those were the primary objections to the application, then they are the principal issues in the case.

Your submissions can bolster the LPA's case. For instance, if the reason for refusing an application was on the grounds that the LPA considered there to be harm to the character of the area, then the views of local residents can help explain this further. What is important to the area? Why do residents feel that a particular development harms the character? Are there particular buildings or views that are important? Or perhaps the application was refused on the grounds of harm to your amenity, in which case you can confirm there would be that harm: eg has the LPA correctly identified the main window that will be affected by a new extension? Have they properly understood how you use your house and garden? Can you reaffirm to the Inspector that sunlight to part of your house really is important to your property?

Although you may have made this general point at the time of the planning application, once you have read why the LPA agrees with this matter then you might be able to provide that extra or specific information to support and expand upon the LPA's conclusion.

You may also need to correct or clarify anything that the LPA has said. They may have made a mistake regarding a matter of fact, or misinterpreted something that you – or others – have written.

Read the appellant's case

It is very important to read the appellant's case at appeal, which can variously be called the Grounds of Appeal or the Appeal Statement. It can be a single document but, in the case of more complex appeals or where there are a number of reasons for refusal, may constitute a number of documents, eg statements relating to highway safety, or trees, or ecology, or whatever the issues may be.

The appellant must submit this case with the lodging of the appeal and a copy must be sent to the LPA. They will have it either at their offices or on their website, usually uploaded alongside the planning application documents. The Statement (and any other documents) will be setting out why the appellant believes planning permission should be granted: it will respond directly to the LPA's reasons for refusal and neighbours' objections, and quite likely provide new evidence. Yet it is surprising how many objectors fail to read these documents before making their own submission at the appeal stage. There is new information here, so you need to read it before preparing your own new submission.

Your new objection letter therefore needs to respond directly to what is in the appellant's submissions. Questions to think about are:

- What is the appellant's justification for the proposed development in light of the reasons for refusal? Why do you not agree with this? The appellant is likely to have provide some specific and detailed analysis of the LPA's case, so you are entitled to similarly carry out a detailed counter-argument to the appellant's case.
- Is there additional evidence the appellant has submitted? If so, you can dispute it. Provide your own contrary evidence if necessary. If you are doing this, make sure that – as with when you were writing to the LPA – your letter to the Inspectorate contains everything the Inspector will need to read or see without having to seek further information. For instance, if the appellant provides evidence on, say, levels of car parking in the area then, if you do not agree, you will need to provide the data to show why: it is not sufficient just to assert your different opinion.
- Is the appellant pointing to other examples of development they think supports their case? If you think those examples are not comparable then explain exactly why not. You may also have your own examples, or precedents, of examples that you consider indicate permission should be refused. If you wish to draw the attention of the Inspector to other examples, again make sure that your submission includes all the information the Inspector needs eg the location of the example and copies of the relevant decision and plans; you cannot assume the Inspector will be aware of any background information.

- Does the appellant attack your original letter that you sent to the LPA? If so, do not take it too personally; the appeal system is adversarial. You should provide any counter arguments to why the appellant's criticism of your case is not justified.
- Do you think the Inspector would benefit from viewing the appeal site from your land? You are allowed to ask the Inspector to come onto your land, or into your home, if you think he/she needs to appreciate a particular point, for example overlooking from a window, or the bulk of an extension, or the proximity to one of your trees. The Inspector is not obliged to agree to this request, though; it is more likely if the LPA's reasons for refusal included harm to something concerning your land or home. If you do make a request to view from your land then also ask to be informed of the date of the site visit, and be prepared to be around for that visit (see later in this chapter).

If you have been informed that the appeal is proceeding by way of a Hearing or Inquiry and you want to attend that event then you should request the Inspectorate to inform you of the date and time. A Hearing or Inquiry allows you to make further submissions to the Inspector in person.

If you want to be directly informed of the outcome of the appeal then you should make that clear in your letter to the Inspectorate, as the LPA does not always tell objectors of the outcome.

Reconsider your case. But also stick to your guns

Things may have changed since the time you wrote to the LPA with your objections to the planning application. This may be physical features on the site, eg new buildings, or landscaping, or a different pattern of use on the land or the highway. Or there may be a change in planning policies.

Events during the course of the planning application and the lodging of the appeal may also make you reconsider your case. For example, the LPA, in assessing the application, may have set out reasons why they did not concur with a particular objection and so did not refuse the application on that ground. Or, conversely, they may have raised an issue you had not originally been aware of. Alternatively, perhaps the appellant may have responded to your objection by modifying the proposed development during the course of the application.

You should, therefore, look objectively at the situation and consider whether your original objections still stand. If you think something different has happened that means a particular concern of yours no longer really applies, or is likely to be a very minor issue, then it may not be worth persisting with that line of objection at the appeal stage. It could possibly be seen as diluting other more substantial and relevant objections. But the opposite situation might also apply: if there has been a change in circumstances, or the LPA objected to a point that you were not initially aware of, then you can expand on that in your objection at the appeal stage.

You are, though, also entitled to stick to your guns with your original objection points. At appeal the Inspector is entitled to reverse or vary any part of the decision of the LPA (whether the appeal relates to that part or not). Effectively the case is dealt with as if it was a planning application made to the Inspector in the first instance. Although the Inspector most commonly sees the primary issues at appeal to be the same as those set out by the LPA in their reasons for refusing planning permission, he or she can refuse permission on any other ground. The Inspector is unlikely to raise issues that no one else has referred to. But, as a third party with an interest in the appeal, if you refer to an issue in your letter of objection at the appeal stage then that is fair territory for the Inspector to consider.

Thus, even though the LPA may not have refused permission on a point that you included in your original objection letter at the planning application stage, the Inspector can refuse permission on those grounds. Clearly, to persuade the Inspector to agree with your case for dismissing the appeal on a ground that the LPA did not raise means you need to put a good case.

Non-determination appeals

An appeal against the LPA's failure to determine a planning application within the required time period is slightly different to other appeals. In this instance there is no formal Decision Notice setting out why the LPA finds the application objectionable. Hence, the appellant may not provide much in the way of an Appeal Statement since they are simply seeking the Inspector to determine whether planning permission is granted, rather than the LPA. However, an appeal against non-determination can occur when the appellant is anticipating a refusal, and so their Appeal Statement may well include additional information over and above that which was provided with the lodging of the planning application.

You should, therefore, still read the appellant's appeal submissions and respond to those if relevant. It is likely that, with no decision from the LPA, your letter of objection to the Planning Inspectorate will involve more reiteration of your original case than in the instance where there has been a refusal of planning permission.

Example letter 1

This example continues from the letter contained in Chapter 2 earlier, and imagines the planning application for 5 houses on a site within a village which was refused permission by the LPA. You had been concerned with the effect on character, highways and flooding, and the LPA refused permission on highways and flooding, but not character.

A Smith
18 Beech Drive
Anytown
A12 3BC

12 November

FAO Case Officer
Temple Quay House, 2 The Square
Temple Quay, Bristol
BS1 6PN

Planning appeal ref: APP/A1234/B/56/7891011.
Land to the rear of 35-39 Beech Drive, Anytown

I live close to the above appeal site and wrote to set out my objections at the time of the planning application (letter dated ../../....)

[Reference your previous letter to be sure the Inspector knows he/she has it.]

I support the refusal of planning permission and confirm my objection to the proposed development on the grounds of a harmful impact on the character of the area, the impact on highway safety and parking, and flooding.

Effect on character of the area

The planning application was not refused on the grounds of harm to the character of the area. However, this remains an objection to the scheme.

My previous letter described the character of the area. The appeal site is within an area of consistent appearance and the land behind the frontage of development is open and undeveloped.

[Add further description here if relevant. Do not just duplicate everything you have said in your previous letter to the LPA, but there may be points you wish to particularly emphasise.]

The proposed development would see 5 houses in a cul-de-sac on this open and undeveloped land. The appellant has said this would be in character with the area because of the position of the houses and their design. However, new houses on the site would be different to the existing layout of the street and appear intrusive to the character

[Add more on the harm that relates back to your earlier outline of the character and respond directly to what the appellant has said in support of their scheme.]

The appellant has referred in their Appeal Statement to a cul-de-sac of housing that was permitted earlier this year at 2-6 Lime Avenue, and says this shows that development to the rear of frontage houses are in character with the area. However, Lime Avenue is a road with a much greater diversity of housing types and has historically had houses set behind the main building frontage. This other example is not comparable to the very consistent character in Beech Drive.

[This paragraph imagines that the appellant has pointed to another development to support their case. If you think there are differences in the cases then you need to explain why. The Inspector will not necessarily know the full details of that case, in which case you can enclose photographs of the other example to show the differences, or other information such as the plans approved by the LPA]

The appellant has not referred to the recent example of planning permission being refused for the erection of 3 houses to the rear of 75-77 Beech Drive (ref. AA/3456), which I referred to in my previous letter. This was partly on the grounds of harm to the character of the area due to the layout of the new houses and enclosed is a copy of the refused plans and Decision Notice. It can be seen that the layout is very similar to the current appeal scheme, with houses in the backland location. The Planning Committee has said in the current appeal that there is greater spacing than in this refused scheme at 75-77 Beech Drive, but it can be seen there is only a marginal difference in the gaps between houses. I therefore believe there would be a cramped appearance to the current appeal scheme.

[In the previous example letter sent to the LPA it was imagined that there was a precedent that assisted your argument. If you want to inform the Inspector further with this case then you will need to provide more details; whilst the LPA will have the full details of their own applications, a Planning Inspector will not have those details unless specifically provided to him/her. In this example it is being imagined that the LPA is not objecting on the grounds of character, and so they may possibly not refer to it or provide details to the Inspector. The appellant is also unlikely to provide details as it does not help their case. Therefore, if you think there is a case that assists your objection, it is safest for you to provide those details. You also need to explain why any other case is relevant to your current objections.]

The new housing would therefore harm the character of the area and so conflict with the planning policies that I referred to in my previous letter, namely Policy H1 of the Anytown Local Plan and the Anytown 'Character Area Appraisal' Supplementary Planning Document.

Impact on highway safety and parking

The planning application was refused permission due to increased hazards from vehicles turning onto the busy Beech Drive, and as there would be insufficient car parking for the new houses

I support these reasons for refusal as explained in my previous letter. Beech Drive is very busy and visibility from the proposed site access would be obscured by parked cars and the curve in the road, as shown in the attached photographs.

The appellant's Appeal Statement claims there is little on-street parking in the area, and has included a snap-shot of the situation on one weekday afternoon. However, my own photographs, which are taken over 5 different occasions including in the evening and weekends, show there is heavy on-street parking and congested streets in the area far more widely.

[It can be helpful to provide further evidence to support the reason for refusal set out on the Decision Notice as you may have local knowledge. This example also imagines that the appellant has submitted evidence in an attempt to prove a point, and if you have contrary evidence then it can be submitted; remember to fully explain that evidence so it can be appraised with the independent mind that the Inspector will have].

The proposed development would therefore be harmful to highway safety and the shortfall in parking would lead to traffic congestion, and so there would be conflict with Policies M2 and M3 of the Anytown Local Plan.

Effect on flooding

My previous letter explained that the site is partly liable to flood from the brook at the rear of the site, and I enclosed photographs of flooding with that letter. Planning permission was refused on the grounds of an increase in the risk of flooding to other houses in the area as there was an objection from the Environment Agency.

The risk of flooding remains a concern of mine, and the Inspector is asked to uphold the Environment Agency's objection on this ground.

[If you do not have anything further to add on a matter, which can be the case for technical issues, then you may just want to reiterate your objection and support the refusal on that ground.]

Summary

The application was refused planning permission on the grounds of harm to highway safety and the increased risk to flooding. I also consider there would also be harm to the character of the area due to the layout of the new housing in a road of consistent appearance. There has been a recent refusal for a scheme that I believe is very similar. The Inspector is asked to dismiss the appeal on these grounds.

Yours sincerely

A Smith

Example letter 2

This example also continues from the letter contained in Chapter 2 earlier, and imagines the planning application to extend an existing takeaway and change the opening hours was refused on the grounds of potential noise. The application had originally proposed a large extract flue but this was amended during the course of the application and a small flue proposed, which the LPA found acceptable.

A Smith
20 Chestnut Hill
Anytown
A12 3BC

15 February

FAO Case Officer
Temple Quay House, 2 The Square
Temple Quay, Bristol
BS1 6PN

Planning appeal ref: APP/B9876/A/5432100/.
25 Chestnut Hill, Anytown

I live next to the above appeal site and wrote to set out my objections at the time of the planning application (letter dated ../../....)

[reference your previous letter to be sure the Inspector knows he/she has it.]

I support the refusal of planning permission and confirm my objection to the proposed development on the grounds of harm to my amenity.

When I wrote my previous letter I explained that the existing takeaway is open until 11pm on weekdays and to 11.30pm on Saturdays and that this use already causes noise and disturbance to me. I also explained that the takeaway had been opening until midnight on some occasions, as the applicant had not been keeping to the permitted opening hours. This has continued since writing my letter, and the takeaway now also accepts deliveries up until midnight and this causes extra noise late at night

[The previous letter imagined there had already been some disturbance. If there has been a change in circumstances since your last letter then you can explain this in your letter to the Planning Inspectorate, with evidence if relevant.]

The proposal to further increase the opening hours of the takeaway would be harmful to my amenity. My previous letter explained that my bedroom windows face the takeaway and the delivery area, and so noise is very intrusive to my house when I should expect it to be quiet. I believe it would be helpful for the Inspector to view the takeaway and delivery area from my house, as the relationship to my windows is otherwise not easy to see. Please therefore inform me of the date of the Inspector's site visit so access can be arranged.

[If you think it would be helpful for the Inspector to visit your property to view the appeal site, such as in this example to see how some aspect of your property would relate to the new use, then you need to make the request in writing setting out your reasons.]

The proposed longer opening hours of the takeaway would be very harmful to my amenity due to the increased noise and disturbance, and I therefore support the refusal of planning permission due to the conflict with Policy D3 of the Anytown Local Plan.

The planning application as first submitted showed a large metal flue on the side elevation. I understand this element of the works were removed during the course of the application and now a small flue is shown. I do not have any objection to that revised flue.

[This is imagining a revision during the course of the application that addressed the design and visual impact point that you had raised in your letter to the LPA. If you no longer object to an element of the scheme then you can say that to indicate you are not objecting to everything for the sake of objecting].

However, my objection on the increased noise and disturbance due to the longer opening hours remains, and the Inspector is asked to dismiss the appeal.

Yours sincerely

A Smith

AFTER SUBMITTING YOUR OBJECTION LETTER

The involvement of third parties in written representation appeals is very limited after the deadline has passed for the submission of a letter of objection to the Planning Inspectorate. There is more involvement at Hearings and Inquires. The stages following the submission of objections are set out below.

Final Comments

Once the deadline for submitting any letters of objection has passed then the Inspectorate send copies of these objections to both the appellant and the LPA. The appellant will also receive any Statement the LPA has made that has responded to their Appeal Statement and evidence they lodged when they made the appeal.

The appellant then has the right of reply to these documents, which is called the 'Final Comments' stage. That is the last stage in the appeal process for Written Representations appeals, ie the appellant has the final say.

The appellant's Final Comments must only comment on what the LPA has said in their Statement and what any third party has said in their submissions to the Inspectorate. No new evidence or issues can be raised, and the Inspectorate are generally diligent in enforcing that rule: any new evidence would be returned to the appellant.

However, you may wish to check the appellant's Final Comments. Your LPA should upload that to their website as a document on the case file soon after receiving it. If you consider they have included new material or are claiming something that is not correct in response to what you have written then you may be able to draw that to the attention of the Inspectorate. However, if you just disagree with a matter of opinion on something then there is not any mileage in raising it: the facts and views are now in front of the Inspector, and it is for him/her to determine the appeal.

EXCEPTIONAL CIRCUMSTANCES

Although the appeals system runs under strict deadlines and rules for the submission of evidence, the Inspectorate recognise that there may be exceptional circumstances that mean representations are necessary outside that timetable. That might be due to personal circumstances, eg health issues, being away, etc. The Inspectorate may take that into account in meeting deadlines. But there could be a change in circumstances that affect how issues in the case should be seen. For instance, if there is a change in planning policy that occurs after the submission of your representation that you consider is relevant to the case. Or there may be a change in, say, the occupancy of a building, or the use of land, or a highway junction in the area.

If you think there is something new that the Inspector should be aware of then you can write to the Inspectorate asking for this change in circumstance to be taken into account. They may not be obliged to accept it, but may agree it is relevant. If so, it is likely they will ask the appellant and the LPA for their views on the matter too.

KEY POINTS

- An appeal is determined by an independent Planning Inspectorate, who is not connected to the LPA or from the local area. They determine the case afresh and so can consider all issues. Although the principal issues are likely to be the LPA's reasons for refusal, this means that the Inspector can come to different conclusions on other points too.
- The LPA will inform previous objectors of an appeal having been lodged. But anyone can write into an appeal (except for HAS/CAS appeals).
- All appeals except HAS/CAS cases allow for additional representations to be made. But there are strict deadlines for submission that must be met. Reminders are not sent about these deadlines, so you - and anyone else such as neighbours or other interested parties - must ensure you write to the Planning Inspectorate by those deadlines.

6. How to be involved at a planning appeal Site Visit, Hearing or Inquiry

In this section you will learn:

- Representing yourself in front of a Planning Inspector at Site Visits, Hearings and Inquiries.
- Costs awards in planning appeals.

Most planning appeals are determined through the Written Representations procedure where, as an objector, your involvement will most commonly be the ability to write an additional objection letter (except for the HAS/CAS cases, as explained). However, almost all appeals also involve a visit to the site from the Planning Inspector. And more complex appeals may run through the Hearing or Public Inquiry procedures. This section of the book explains how you can be involved in these.

The Inspector's site visit

After the final exchange of all written documentation then the Inspectorate arrange a visit to the appeal site for the Planning Inspector. The appellant and the LPA are informed of the date and time for this, but neighbours will only be directly informed if they have asked the Inspectorate in advance. Site visits take place during working hours on weekdays.

The site visit procedure will depend on the submissions by the appellant and the LPA regarding whether the visit needs to enter private land. If that is the case then an 'access required' site visit is arranged and the appellant is required to provide that access. The LPA is not required to attend the site visit. If the appeal site can be seen from public land then an 'unaccompanied' site visit is arranged.

A site visit is usually a fairly formal affair, and led by the Inspector. He or she will know what they want to see on the site. The appellant will have been informed beforehand that the site visit is not the opportunity to discuss the merits of the case with the Inspector: the decision is based on the written submissions, and the site visit is there for the Inspector to see the physical features of the site and surroundings.

If you have requested the Inspector to view from your land or property then, as mentioned previously, it is up to the Inspector to agree to that request; they are not obliged to go onto your land. If they do want to enter your land then they will most likely inform you at the time of the site visit itself: typically after seeing the appeal site then the Inspector will know whether it would be helpful to their decision to also go onto your land. This means they will usually knock on your door to inform you at the time. However, if you see the Inspector on public land, eg the pavement, then you could ask them if they intend to visit.

Alternatively, the LPA may have made a specific request for the Inspector to view from your land. This will have been indicated to the Inspectorate on their Appeal Questionnaire at the start of the appeal process, and is typically done where the LPA are particularly concerned about some effect on your land. If this is the case then the Inspector is likely to want to view from your land and, if you are concerned with the appeal proposal, you should try to ensure you are around for the site visit.

If the Inspector does come to your land or property then the visit will be run in the same fashion as when they enter the appeal site. They are not there to discuss the merits of the case but just to see physical features (though there can be the opportunity to discuss the case at a Hearing or Inquiry site visit; see later in this Chapter). The Inspector may be content to enter your land by himself/herself, but may consider that in the interests of fairness, the appellant needs to accompany them onto your land. You are not obliged to let the appellant onto your land, but be aware that if the Inspector says he/she only wants to come onto your land with the appellant and you refuse, then it is most likely the Inspector will decide not to visit you.

Although the Inspector knows what to look for at a site visit, and the event is quite formalised, you should ensure that if the Inspector does come onto your land then he/she does not depart without seeing everything you wish to be seen. You are allowed to check the Inspector has viewed everything you have referred to in your submissions: both on the site and in the wider area, if you have already mentioned that.

If you are expecting the Inspector to visit your land or property at the site visit there are some general tips.

Dos

- Do try to ensure you can attend the time of the site visit, particularly if the LPA have asked the Inspector to view from your property. If you cannot make it personally, is there a friend or relative who can attend? They only have to let the Inspector onto the land, and Inspectors are familiar with the person attending a site visit not being the person who wrote to them.
- Do refresh yourself with the scheme drawings and all documentation, so you are ready to answer any questions if the Inspector asks.
- Do be confident to ask that the Inspector has all the right drawings and documents.
- Do be aware of how the Inspector wants to run the site visit - it varies. Some like to walk around by themselves, others may wish to have matters explained to them. So don't impose on the Inspector if they want to be alone.

- Do point out any physical features on the site that you want the Inspector to see, but don't make any subjective comment on issues. For instance, you could say 'This is the window closest to the proposed extension I referred to in my letter', but you could not say 'You can see how close the extension would be to this window which means there would be overlooking all the time, and reduced sunlight all through the afternoon and into the evening'.
- Do ensure you are happy the Inspector has seen everything on the site before he/she leaves.

Don'ts

- Don't complain and grumble about how the LPA may have handled the planning application, or at the appellant for putting in the planning application! The Inspector has arrived to look at the site and judge the current appeal.
- Don't be offended if the Inspector refuses even simple hospitality.
- Don't try to give any extra evidence at the site visit, such as documents or photographs. It will be rejected.

PREPARING FOR A HEARING OR INQUIRY

As explained previously, the procedures for Written Representation appeals, Hearings and Inquires are generally the same in the stages up to the date of the Hearing/Inquiry itself as each route allows for you to make a written submission in response to the appellant's initial case. The Hearing and Inquiry, though, both involve the chance to further make any case through oral submissions to the Inspector, and you are entitled to attend these events.

Hearing

A Hearing is an informal discussion, led by the Inspector. If you have asked to be informed of the Hearing then the Inspectorate will write to you letting you know the date, time and venue.

The Inspector will have produced an agenda that list the topics to be discussed at the Hearing. These are most likely to be based on the reasons for refusal set out on the LPA's decision notice and the evidence set out in the appellant's Appeal Statement. The appellant and the LPA will also have been expected to produce a Statement of Common Ground before the Hearing which sets out the matters that are not in dispute.

You are able to add any other topics to the Inspector's agenda at the Hearing. You want to ensure that everything relevant to your concerns is discussed. However, the Hearing is not an opportunity to submit additional evidence that should have been included within your appeal submissions; the Inspector will be strict about any attempt to slip through the strict deadlines on submission of evidence by all parties, unless there are very good reasons.

After the Inspector introduces a topic for discussion, he/she will ask the appellant for their view on that topic. The LPA will reply verbally with their opinion. You, as a third party, are then allowed to comment. The appellant then has the verbal right of reply. The Inspector may follow this process with direct questions to any party.

The process can be slightly stilted and perhaps less informal than the Hearing system was intended to be, due to the convention of statements and rights of reply being followed. If you consider your point has not been covered then this means you need to be bold in speaking up: it can be the case that the discussion moves on to a new topic with you realising that not everything has been covered, or that a full response to the appellant or the LPA has not been given. You do not want to leave a Hearing thinking there were gaps in the discussion.

The key to a Hearing is preparation. You will have produced your own representations at the application stage and again at the appeal stage. You will have read the appellant's Appeal Statement, and also seen the LPA's Statement. There may be other documents too from third parties, such as the Environment Agency, or the Highways Authority, or other neighbours and landowners. You should therefore read all that documentation carefully in order to be ready to make your case, and so any verbal submission from others is less likely to be a surprise. Make notes on your case to ensure on the day you are ready to cover everything that you want to say, and you know what the appellant is likely to say.

The Hearing will usually reconvene on the same day as a site visit. This is accompanied by both the appellant and a representative from the LPA, and discussions may continue on the site. You, as a third party, may ask to be present at the site visit. However, if the appeal site is private land the appellant is not obliged to allow access, although they typically do.

Inquiries

If the appeal is following the Inquiry route then the date of the Inquiry takes on a particular significance. As with the Hearing, the Inspectorate will inform you of the date. This will have been in consultation with the appellant and the LPA, since there is likely to be legal representation and so a number of different people to coordinate.

Once the Inquiry date is set, then the Inspectorate will inform the appellant and the LPA of the date for the submission of 'Proofs of Evidence', which is 4 weeks before the date of the Inquiry. A Proof of Evidence is essentially a detailed Statement of Case, and so is likely to expand in even greater detail the matter first raised in the Appeal Statements by both parties. The Proofs may cover a number of topics, eg town planning matters, trees, highways, noise. A Statement of Common Ground is also produced.

The process at an Inquiry is very formalised. There are likely to be formal opening statements by legal representatives, and then evidence is presented verbally with formal cross-examination by advocates. The Inspector will also take an inquisitorial role and is likely to ask questions to anyone who gives formal evidence.

Third parties may appear at the Inquiry to present evidence. This is most commonly in a less formal role than the main parties. They will typically be given time to put their views orally to the Inspector on the topics where they have an interest. If you wish to participate then you should ensure you attend the beginning of the Inquiry – they can stretch over days – to let the Inspector know of your intentions. The Inspector is usually accommodating to objectors who want to speak and will ensure a mutually convenient time to all parties for your involvement.

As with a Hearing, preparation is key for an Inquiry. You will need to be very familiar with your representations, and you should read the other parties' submissions as well. You are likely to be questioned on your views – probably not as intensely as the main parties of the appellant and the LPA – but you need to be familiar with what are the issues under consideration.

As with a Hearing, there is a site visit at an Inquiry, where there may be continued discussions regarding the case.

Third parties are allowed to take a more active role in Inquiries by requesting 'Rule 6' status. This might typically occur for local community groups or parish councils; it is rare for individuals to have this status. This makes you a main party at the Inquiry with the right to submit Proofs of Evidence, be part of any cross-copying of other parties' Proofs and Statements, and participate fully in the Inquiry event itself including the right to cross-examine other parties. If you wish to have Rule 6 status then you need to contact the Planning Inspectorate at the very beginning of the Inquiry timetable. If you wish to do this then it is advisable to seek professional advice on Rule 6 status from a solicitor or planning consultant.

COSTS IN PLANNING APPEALS

The appeal process is the one area of the planning system where costs can be awarded. However, unlike the Courts system, costs do not automatically follow the decision, ie the appellant is not simply awarded costs from the LPA if they win the appeal. The objective of the costs regime is to encourage reasonable behaviour by all parties, to ensure a timely and efficient appeal process.

This means that costs are only awarded if there has been unreasonable behaviour by any party, and if that behaviour has led to an unnecessary appeal or wasted time. This includes third parties, ie objectors to appeals. It is rare for costs to be awarded against third parties, particularly at Written Representation appeals, but to minimise the risk of this you should ensure you do not behave in an unreasonable manner. The Government provides guidance on what might constitute such behaviour, and this typically includes:

- lack of co-operation with the main parties during an appeal, particularly at Hearings or Inquires, with a delay in providing information or keeping to deadlines
- introducing fresh and substantial evidence at a late stage in the appeal process that leads to an adjournment at a Hearing or an Inquiry
- providing information that is shown to be manifestly inaccurate or untrue, or the deliberate concealment of relevant evidence

This is not an exhaustive list, but provided you behave reasonably during the appeal process and stick to the Inspectorate's guidance and deadlines then you are at little risk of costs being awarded against you.

KEY POINTS

- Your representations at the appeal stage should not just be a resubmission of what you wrote to the LPA during the planning application stage. The appellant will have written a Statement of Case that has responded to the reasons for refusal, and there may be additional evidence on other matters. Read that before writing your new letter and respond to their case.
- Hearings and Inquiries allow you to present your case in person to the Planning Inspector. If you want to be involved in those events then let the Inspectorate know and you will be allowed to participate. Prepare thoroughly in advance of the event.
- If you think it would be helpful to the Inspector to enter your land or property at the appeal site visit then you can write to request that. Site visits are carried out with certain formalities, so make sure you are aware of those.
- Although rare, costs can be awarded against third parties in appeals. Make sure that does not happen to you by ensuring you behave reasonably and comply with any rules, guidance or deadlines given to you by the Planning Inspectorate.

7. What happens after an appeal is decided

In this section you will learn:

- The possible outcomes of a planning appeal.
- What you can do, depending on those outcomes.

After the site visit, regardless of the process, in due course the Inspector will issue the decision on the appeal. The length of time for this decision varies with the type of case: typically around a month, but will be longer for more complex Hearings or Inquiries.

The Inspector's decision will either allow the appeal or dismiss it, and is written in the form of a letter that explains in detail the reason the appeal is allowed or dismissed. If you have included in your letter to the Inspectorate that you want to be informed of the decision direct then that will be sent to you. But also keep a check on the LPA's website and on the Appeals Casework Portal.

AN ALLOWED APPEAL

There is no right of further appeal against the Inspector's decision merely because you disagree with the decision. There is only a right for a High Court challenge against a decision if it can be proven the Inspector made an error in law, eg misinterpreting or misapplying a policy, or failing to take account of an important consideration, and the High Court must be persuaded that such an event might have affected the outcome of the decision. A challenge must be made within 42 days of the date of the decision.

If the High Court decides there was an error in law then the appeal is returned to the Planning Inspectorate for re-determination. This does not necessarily mean a different decision is reached, as the appeal is simply looked at afresh.

This means that, if the appeal is allowed, you can only get it overturned through the Courts. Due to the complex legal issues in this course of action, and the likely high costs, legal advice should always be sought if a High Court challenge is considered as this book cannot cover all possible matters.

Minor errors in the decision

Occasionally an Inspector may make a minor error in the decision, eg a drafting error that cites the wrong application number, an incorrect reference to approved plans, the wrong address etc. These may not materially affect the decision, but you might consider they cause some issues for you in the future, eg if the appeal is allowed but there is some discrepancy in the listed drawing numbers, which might lead to confusion at a later date as to what is the approved scheme.

In the past, these errors, although minor, could also only have been corrected through the High Court. But fortunately now the Inspectorate is allowed to correct these through what is known as the 'Slip Rule'. If there is a simple error that can be corrected then you might wish to write to the Inspectorate requesting a change, and this must be done within 42 days of the decision letter.

A DISMISSED APPEAL

If the appeal has been dismissed, then the appellant can also only have it overturned through the Courts if there has been an error in law, not just because they disagree with the Inspector's judgement. If there are no grounds for challenge then that is the end of the road for that particular application. But it does not necessarily mean the appellant can do nothing else. As an Inspector's decision is usually detailed, and sets out what are the shortcomings of a scheme and where there is conflict with planning policies, an appellant may choose to rework the development proposal and go back to the LPA with a new application that they believe addresses the Inspector's concerns. They are allowed to do this and you will need to engage with the new planning application in the same way as before: it is back to square one for writing your objection letter.

KEY POINTS

- A planning appeal decision – whether allowed or dismissed – can only be challenged in the High Court on matters of law. Neither the appellant nor you can appeal again purely on the grounds that you disagree with the Planning Inspector. If you think there has been an error in law then you should seek legal advice if you are considering a challenge.
- The Inspector's appeal decision is in the form of a letter that sets out why he/she considers it accords with relevant planning policies and other material considerations, or why it does not. If the appeal is dismissed this may mean that an appellant feels they can overcome the Inspector's concerns by submitting a fresh planning application to the LPA, in which case the whole process of planning application procedures starts again.

8. Ready to write?

Being notified of a planning application can come as a surprise: you receive a letter through the door from the Council, or see a notice on a lampost, or your neighbour tells you. There are strict time limits for making your views known, but you do not want to rush in and write about irrelevant matters, or miss the chance to mention important points. The advice in this book will help you be focused on how you can get your objections across to the planning officers and to the Councillors who will be determining that planning application.

A planning appeal has an even stricter procedure and deadlines for making representations. Remember that the process is different from a planning application – you are not just repeating everything you said at the application stage – and this book has told you how to frame your further objections, and how to engage with the Planning Inspectorate to make your views known.

Involvement in a planning application and appeal can be a long process. There can be the need to make a number of objection letters when the application is running – if there is new information or amendments from the applicant, and when the application comes to Committee – and then the appeal process means more letters. And even if a planning application is refused, or appeal dismissed, then it may all start again, with a new planning application submitted. You will need to keep up the effort and, with the help of this book, make your case effectively.

9. Using professionals

This book has set out how to prepare and submit your own objection to a planning application or planning appeal. You may need the help of professionals in the appeal to make the best case. This is particularly the case if there are technical issues raised in the planning application, such as:

- **Arboriculturists** to address tree issues
- **Drainage consultants,** for matters such as sustainable drainage, flooding
- **Highways consultants,** who can advise on safe access, parking provision, traffic generation
- **Surveyors,** who can provide evidence on structural issues, day and sunlight, access and boundary matters
- **Noise consultants,** if issues relate to impact of a scheme on you
- **Air quality consultants,** where the quality of the surrounding environment or internal space is a concern
- **Ecologists**, whose expertise is likely if there is any issue relating to protected species
- **Energy consultants,** as LPAs are increasingly aware of the need to minimise the use of energy
- **Solicitors** will be necessary for legal agreements, and advice on matters relating to legal precedent

You can of course pass the appeal over to a professional agent to handle from beginning to end, and such a role is commonly undertaken by solicitors, town planning consultants or architects.

10. Glossary

Commercial appeals service (CAS)
A planning appeal for small commercial developments, which runs under the Planning Inspectorate's fast-track programme

Conservation Area
An area of land that is designated by an LPA as being of special architectural or historic interest, whose character or appearance they wish to preserve or enhance. A designated area of land can vary in size and by what type of land, water or buildings are covered

Decision Notice
The formal decision by an LPA on a planning application that grants permission or refuses permission

Delegated Report
The detailed report on a planning application that is written by the planning case officer

Development plan
The plan produced by an LPA that sets out policies against which any development proposal will be judged. It may comprise a number of adopted documents, including local plans, neighbourhood plans and spatial strategies

Final comments
The stage during a planning appeal where the appellant has the right of reply to the LPA's appeal statement and any submissions by third parties

Hearing
The route for a planning appeal which involves the exchange of written submissions and then an informal hearing session chaired by the Planning Inspector, which allows for a discussion of the appeal

Heritage asset
A building, monument, site, place, area or landscape identified as having a degree of significance meriting consideration in planning decisions because of its heritage interest. This may include assets designated by bodies such as Historic England, eg listed buildings, and also those identified by the LPA, eg locally listed buildings.

Householder appeals service (HAS)
A planning appeal for extensions and alterations to single family houses, which runs under the Planning Inspectorate's fast-track programme

Inquiry
The route for a planning appeal which involves the exchange of written submissions, the submitting of Proofs of Evidence, and then a formal Inquiry with the Planning Inspector and usually legal representation

Legal agreement
An agreement entered under s106 of the Town and Country Planning Act 1990 to mitigate the impacts of a development proposal. Can also be called a planning obligation, a Unilateral Undertaking, or a s106 agreement, depending on the format of the agreement.

Listed building
A building that has been identified for its special architectural or historic interest. Works to that building are the subject of additional protection and needs consent under the Planning (Listed Buildings and Conservation Act) 1990, but the LPA must also have regard to development that affects the setting of a listed building.

Local Plan
See Development plan

LPA
Abbreviation for local planning authority, which is the public authority which undertakes the planning authority for a particular area. This is typically the district, borough or metropolitan council, but will include, in various parts of the country, the county council, Broads Authority, National Park Authority, the Mayor of London or a development corporation.

National Planning Policy Framework (NPPF)
The Government's policy on planning, which can be a material consideration in all planning decisions undertaken by an LPA

Non-determination appeal
An appeal lodged following the failure of the LPA to determine a planning application within the statutory timescale

Planning Committee Report
The detailed report on a planning application that is written by the planning case officer for the purposes of the relevant Committee of the LPA. It will usually set out a recommendation to approve or refuse planning permission, with the final decision made by the Members of that Committee.

Planning Inspector
A person appointed by the Secretary of State for Housing, Communities and Local Government to determine a planning appeal

Planning Inspectorate
The Government agency that runs the planning appeal system. Liaison between appellants, LPAs and third parties is with an allocated case officer at the Planning Inspectorate.

Planning Practice Guidance
The Government's guidance on specific planning issues, including heritage, noise, trees, flooding.

Representation
A general term for any submissions made by main parties, or third parties, to a planning application or appeal. It is a neutral term, as representations may be made in support or opposition. Hence, if you have objected to an application or appeal, you may have it referred to just as a representation.

Site visit
The visit to the site by the planning case officer. At appeal, the Inspector will also visit the site, either through an Unaccompanied Site Visit (which is viewing only from public land) or an Access Required Site Visit (where the Inspector will enter the appeal site)

Statutory period
The time period within which an LPA must determine the planning application

Supplementary Planning Document (SPD)
A document produced by the LPA which adds further detail to the policies in the development plan, eg guidance for development on specific sites, or on particular issues such as design. Supplementary planning documents (SPDs) can be a material consideration in planning decisions but are not part of the development plan.

Third parties
A person, or group, who has an interest in a planning application or appeal who is not one of the main two parties: the LPA and the applicant/appellant. As an objector, you are a third party.

Written Representations
The route for a planning appeal which involves the exchange of written submissions, followed by the Inspector's site visit.

Printed in Great Britain
by Amazon

32896708R00064